Interpretations in English

David Aldred, Tony Bulger, Gethin Evans

from an original concept by Michel Bellity

CASSELL

CASSELL PUBLISHERS LIMITED
Artillery House, Artillery Row
London SW1P 1RT

© Cassell Publishers Limited 1989

All rights reserved. This book is protected by copyright. No part of it may be reproduced, stored in a retrieval system, or transmitted in any form or by any means, electronic, mechanical, photocopying, recording or otherwise, without written permission from the Publishers.

First published 1989
Reprinted 1990 (twice)

British Library Cataloguing in Publication Data

Aldred, David
   Interpretations in English
   1. English language – For schools
   I. Title II. Evans, G. R. (Gethin Richard), *1948–1988*
   III. Bulger, Tony
   428
   ISBN 0-304-31766-7

Printed and bound in Great Britain by Courier International Ltd, Tiptree, Essex

The Publishers are grateful for permission to include material from the following sources and organisations

The Labour Research Department for cartoons by Roger Evans

Friends of The Earth and Fred Pine for a cartoon that appeared in *Earth Matters*

The *Financial Times* for an article on women in Italy

Manchester City Council for statistics

A. M. Heath and Secker and Warburg for a quotation from *Animal Farm* by George Orwell

Culture and Society by Raymond Williams published by Chatto and Windus

2001: A Space Odyssey by Stanley Kubrik and Arthur C. Clarke published by Century Hutchinson

Housewife by Anne Oakley published by Pelican Books

Manchester in the Victorian Age by Gary S. Messinger published by Manchester University Press

Moscow Women by Carola Hansson and Karin Liden published by W. H. Allen

Popular Computing Weekly for a cartoon

Social Structure by George P. Murdock published by Macmillan Publishing Company

Hostage Bound, Hostage Free by Benjamin Weir published by the Lutterworth Press

Marilyn Martin-Jones, University of Lancaster for the reproduction of an extract of a letter to *The Guardian*

The Pelican History of the World by J. M. Roberts published by Century Hutchinson Ltd

Jogging with Clients by Len Collinson published by Colgran Publications

Poverty and Inequality in Common Market Countries edited by Vic George and Roger Lawson published by Routledge and Kegan Paul

Saatchi and Saatchi for an advertisement

Greenpeace, the Press Association and the British Army for photographs

Great care has been taken to trace the ownership of material used in this book. The Publishers will welcome information that will enable them to rectify any errors or omissions.

Illustrated by Julie Ellis
Original cartoon ideas by Lexis
Designed by Lexis

Dedication

This book is dedicated to the memory of

Gethin Richard Evans

1948 – 1988

who made much of it possible with his original insights and valuable contributions

Contents

Introduction		vi
Unit 1	A Question of Class	1
Unit 2	Housewives' Choice?	9
Unit 3	The Fourth Estate	19
Unit 4	Television is Watching You!	25
Unit 5	Soft Sell	33
Unit 6	Murderers or Martyrs?	41
Unit 7	Defence of the Realm	47
Unit 8	This is I.T.!	55
Unit 9	Training for Life?	63
Unit 10	Tomorrow's World?	71
Grammar Exercises		77
Listening: Tape Transcripts		87
Grammar Exercises: Keys		98

Introduction

Foreword *Interpretations in English* is a resource book for use with upper-intermediate and advanced students of English as a foreign language, covering a wide range of topics of general interest to the student studying at home or abroad.

The material included in this book is intended to introduce a contemporary journalistic style of English as it is used in the 'real world', to stimulate lively debate in the classroom, and to motivate students to do, where possible, a little research of their own. The texts reflect a variety of fact and opinion that the teacher may also use as starting points for more extended project work. A range of exercises and activities is suggested, but there is plenty of scope for you to exploit the material to suit the varying needs of your students and to take into account different teaching methodologies.

Each unit has an *input phase* followed by an *output/feedback phase*. The structure of the units is as follows:

Input Phase

Visual Introduction

The introductory visual images should be used as a stimulus for preliminary questions and answers and as a basis for any pre-teaching you feel is necessary for your students to tackle the unit. Of course, you may have access to other photographs or pictures that will further attract the students' attention to the topic area of the unit.

Pre-text Questions

Some simple questions are posed before each unit. This means that students are reading for information from the outset.

It is not necessary for students to understand the text completely before answering these very generalised questions. Students may well have an opinion on these before even looking at the text, in which case it can be valuable to note down people's immediate reactions on the board in advance of studying the text and return to them later.

Main Text The language used in the main text of each unit is a fairly sophisticated, natural style of English commonly found in periodicals and newspapers. The language is therefore not graded from unit to unit and is not specially adapted for foreigners. Initially, you may decide to divide the main text into smaller 'chunks' for intensive reading.

You may also choose to pre-teach certain structures or vocabulary that will present problems for your group, or it may be appropriate to talk through some of the main issues using the students' native language if the class is an homogeneous one. Alternatively, with a class who are already quite experienced in reading authentic passages of English, you may prefer to go through the whole text as if it really were a magazine article they were scanning and pick up any difficulties afterwards using the glossary, comprehension questions and translation.

Mini Texts In each unit you will find a number of short texts relating to, but often contrasting with, the main theme of the unit, taking the form of a case study or illustration of the main argument. It may sometimes be appropriate to allow students to tackle these with less teacher-support than the longer first text, individually or in pairs.

Students might eventually write their own short pieces using these as a model; this type of extension exercise is particularly relevant if you produce your own broadsheet or pamphlet on the topic under investigation. If you use the main text for very intensive study you might prefer to ask students just to 'get the gist' of the mini texts to vary the pace of the lesson, and to provide practice in effective scan reading.

Listening It is recommended that the book is used in conjunction with the accompanying cassette where a variety of voices and accents can be found throughout the ten recorded dialogues. A transcript of the content can be found towards the end of the book which may be helpful as a basis for lesson preparation or as a follow-up to hearing the tape. The listening exercises should not, of course, turn into reading practice; it is much more valuable to concentrate on a small part of a dialogue and really get your students using their ears than to ask them to tackle the whole thing with the script before them.

The language on the tape is at natural speed but in a moderately controlled form; the dialogues are assumed to come from media broadcasts and business-like discussions rather than, say, casual conversations between friends. Therefore interruptions and crossovers are minimised, but the language is comparatively sophisticated and often quite concise.

When beginning a listening exercise, it is usually most effective to play the tape several times, in segments if necessary, asking fairly easy questions as you go along. Students can ask each other questions after one of the replays. They should then look at the written questions on the dialogue in the book. You may not wish to allow students to read the transcript of the tape at least until the very end. Depending on your group, you may decide to use the material more intensively by introducing a 'fill in the gaps' type exercise, even a short piece of dictation. Afterwards, some students will enjoy role-plays based on the language of the dialogue, graduating to writing their own conversations; they should be encouraged to do this by the teacher.

Output/Feedback Stage

Grammar Exercises

Teachers requiring formal structural exercises will find these at the back of the book. In each unit a page reference is given immediately after the comprehension questions for the quick location of grammar exercises, often thematically linked to the unit. There are keys or sample answers (where more than one answer is possible) at the very end of the book which can be used by the student for self-correcting.

In many cases these exercises will serve as revision exercises on grammar points the student will have covered previously, eg passivisation, relative clauses, common conditionals etc. As usual, it is up to the teacher to pre-teach or extend these according to the level (and interest) of the class. You may wish to refer to a standard grammar book for a more detailed explanation of the linguistic structures and to provide further examples.

Language Activity

In each unit there are suggestions for other language work in which two or more of the four skills (speaking, listening, reading and writing) are employed. Ensure that, for instance, preparation work for a discussion that involves note-taking is done thoroughly; not only will the talk be more fluent and correct but the student will gain from practising jotting down ideas directly into English. Similarly, ensure that people are listening to a debate if they are not speaking in it; make sure they all contribute at some level even if you have to ask for written summaries of the proceedings.

The idea is to integrate the skills as closely as possible so that the different activities reinforce one another and the new language is rehearsed in different contexts until it can be assimilated.

Media Watch and Questionnaire

For students fortunate enough to be studying in Britain, it is essential to exploit as much as possible any access they have to advertisements, TV programmes, publications etc by drawing their attention to examples of the language and images contained in them. Of course, it is still possible to talk about the mass media in English even if the examples are drawn from Europe. If you are using *Interpretations in English* outside the UK, it is quite often possible to acquire material written in English but even where this proves difficult, students should be encouraged to find material in their own language. You might consider forming your students into groups and using such material as a translation exercise.

Either way, it is extremely valuable if students can be persuaded to go off on their own and report back to the class with their 'findings'; not only does it help the student develop individual learning strategies, but it also means that many examples can be surveyed in class by pooling people's results. If you can establish a genuine 'seminar' atmosphere, where the students inform and question each other, they will quickly gain confidence in their ability to use English in all situations, to gain and give information, to support their arguments, even to recount an amusing experience. Again, a written summary of the research undertaken would consolidate any new language that has been acquired in the course of the survey.

Interpretations in English contains a wide variety of source material that should be of interest for its content as well as for its linguistic style. The texts are intended to offer starting points for smaller and larger scale projects to be undertaken both inside and outside the classroom. We hope you will find it to be a flexible resource that will enrich your English language teaching, whether at home or abroad.

A Question of Class

unit one

A Question of Class

Interpretations in English

A Definition Social class is the grouping of people into categories on the basis of occupation.

However, Raymond Williams in his book *Keywords* identifies another dimension of meaning. He talks about class as implying a formation (a social, cultural and political organisation) that results from the collective consciousness of belonging to a group with common interests.

Some Quotations

1 *Wherever there is great property, there is great inequality... for one very rich man there must be at least five hundred poor.*

and, referring to Britain

2 *...a nation whose government is influenced by shopkeepers.*

Adam Smith (1723 – 1790)

which became, in Napoleon's famous saying

3 *England is a nation of shopkeepers.*

4 *All animals are equal, but some are more equal than others.*

George Orwell

5 *The defect of equality is that we only desire it with our superiors.*

Henry Becque (1837 – 1899)

6 *When Adam delved and Eve span who was then the gentleman?*

Watt Tyler, leader of the Peasants' Revolt 1381

7 *The real ruling class could not be put in question, so they are seen as temporarily absent, or as the good old people succeeded by the bad new people – themselves succeeding themselves.*

Raymond Williams

Glossary **delved** an old word meaning *dug*
span an old word for *spun* ie made cloth by spinning

Questions
a) Explain the connection between property and inequality made in quotation 1.
b) How has the meaning changed from the second to the third quotation?
c) Explain the contradictions in quotations 4 and 5.
d) What is Watt Tyler saying about the nature of man in quotation 6?
e) Why would the ruling class wish to be hidden in quotation 7?

* See how many different ideas of class you can gather from friends and acquaintances. Put these ideas into the form of definitions.

Read through the following text and as you do so try and answer these questions. Remember that you don't have to understand every word in order to give an answer.

1 What exactly is a social class?
2 What new classes can be identified today?

Viewpoints

A The concept of class is a myth invented for political reasons. In reality, Europe is a classless society in the sense that whatever your background or origins it is perfectly possible to rise through the echelons and, in fair competition with your fellow men, reach the top of your chosen career field through talent and hard work alone. Class conflict, if it exists at all, is purely the envy of the work-shy towards those who through sheer hard effort and sacrifice have 'gone for it' and achieved their well-earned reward.

When referring to *class* people are usually trying to instil a sense of guilt in the successful in order to undermine their morale and, through creating an environment that is antithetical to success, attain the political aim of a so-called equal society that would in all probability be based on coercion. Class, then, is keenly grasped by the mediocre and the lazy and used as an ideological weapon to defeat their superiors with whom they cannot compete on the same terms.

To sum up, then, in the western democracy of today it is quite possible for a person of talent born into circumstances of deprivation to achieve wealth and status in later life through initiative and motivation. Conversely, a person born into a privileged environment can easily slip down the social scale if they show an absence of these same characteristics.

B An index to class is the power exercised by the individuals within it over their environment and their lives. Freedom of choice is a result of the freedom of action that comes from being in control of things and not controlled by them. Thus a person who is homeless or hungry cannot be said to be free.

Power influences the position of different groups in society not only in terms of earnings but also in terms of employment, housing, health, education and other socially desirable goods. There is substantial evidence that by and large one type of disadvantage is related to another to create an intricate web of disadvantages. Social, political and economic systems operate in ways which at best modify only slightly and, at worst, exacerbate the disadvantages which low income groups suffer.

The class to which a person belongs in the majority of cases determines the extent and nature of his freedom. This is because economic conditions include and preclude certain courses of action. For example, a pay increase can suddenly make an activity, such as a foreign holiday, affordable that was previously impossible to finance. If a considerable proportion of a life is spent in taking care of very basic needs such as eating, housing, clothing, and warmth how can that individual find expression in cultural contexts?

However, many people from working class backgrounds have attained positions of influence by working in areas such as the Trade Union movement that, in many ways, challenge the establishment. It is often the case that those who have moved beyond their class of origin are keenest to assume the values of the class they join and become the strongest proponents of the status quo which afforded them the opportunity for advancement and has bestowed on them the fruits of success. As individuals are absorbed by the establishment they gradually succumb to its temptations and even sometimes (for example Hugh Scanlon, Frank Chapple and Len Murray) accept membership of the House of Lords.

Class differences in society are mirrored in differences between nations and groups of nations, for example, the developed world, the developing world and the third world. Even within Europe there is a form of class division between the rich industrial north and the poorer, predominantly agricultural, south and the conflicts of interest are reflected in EEC arguments about levels of agricultural subsidy.

A Question of Class
Interpretations in English

There have been few examples in history of a truly classless society where, to any significant degree, equality of pay and conditions prevailed. Two short-lived examples are the Paris Commune of 1871 which was ruthlessly destroyed by the forces of the French government and the anarchist regime that controlled Barcelona in the early days of the Spanish Civil War which was ironically brought to a violent end by the communists.

Today in Europe there is a new class which is growing apace that has come to be known as the underclass or sub-class. This class consists of groups of individuals who do not have access to the rights enjoyed by members of other social strata. Indeed, in order to secure very basic living conditions taken for granted by others, they are often forced to suffer the indignity of a means test, be at the receiving end of charity and have to rely on run-down public services. The worlds of private transport, private health care, private education and private housing are remote and inaccessible.

The underclass consists of the poor, the homeless, many of the unemployed, the emotionally disturbed, the disabled. A high proportion will be from ethnic minorities, many being employed illegally at low wage levels and under sweatshop conditions. Some will be employed completely illegally; their very existence unrecognised and unrecorded by the authorities. This class also includes drug addicts, prostitutes and alcoholics. The underclass are the unspoken but ever-present shadow of our modern lifestyle.

Whereas the poor of the last century were employed and formed the working class, the poor of today are now largely unemployed and form part of the underclass.

Glossary

echelons	social levels
work-shy	unwilling to make an effort
affordable	within one's financial means
status quo	things as they are
succumb	surrender
grow apace	increase rapidly
sweatshop	place where working conditions are extremely poor and people are forced to work very hard for little pay

Comprehension

1. How, according to Text A, can one become part of a higher class?
2. How is the concept of class used by the untalented against their betters?
3. Explain how a hungry person is automatically in a low class according to the argument of Text B.
4. Explain what is meant by the phrase *cultural contexts*.
5. Give an example of a route by which a working class person can be promoted into a higher class.
6. What was the fate of the two experiments in egalitarianism cited in the text?
7. Comment on the phrase *sub-class*.
8. From the text as a whole, what are the attributes of a member of the *higher* social class?
9. Find a word or phrase in the text which means

beginnings	opposed to
vacation abroad	the most enthusiastic
reflected	levels of society

10 Find an antonym (opposite) in Text A for the following

reality   fall
hard-working   unmerited
opposed to   free will

Exercise

A The following is a list of classes that are often referred to. In pairs re-arrange the list into order according to social hierarchy. Keep together any that you feel are synonyms (have the same meaning).

peasant   ruling class   working class
middle class   upper class   bourgeois
underclass   aristocracy   lower-middle class
privileged   capitalist   petit-bourgeois
merchant   manufacturing   leisured
monarchy   nobility   proletariat

B What occupations would the members of these classes be expected to have? Here are some possibilities

Lawyer   Artist   Assembly worker
Accountant   Hospital porter Labourer
Engineer   Nurse   Entrepreneur
Chef   Teacher   Politician
Programmer   Farm worker   Fitter

Manchester Yesterday

1 One day I walked with one of these middle-class gentlemen into Manchester. I spoke to him about the disgraceful unhealthy slums and drew his attention to the disgusting condition of that part of town in which the factory workers lived. I declared that I had never seen so badly built a town in my life. He listened patiently and at the corner of the street at which we parted company he remarked: 'And yet there is a great deal of money made here. Good morning, Sir.'

from *The Condition of the Working Class in England* by Friedrich Engels 1845

Images of Naples

2 If you walk down the Via Roma in Naples today it is striking how the street is lined with shops selling designer goods for the conspicuous consumption of the wealthy while, behind this exterior of affluence, artisans toil in workshops for low wages to produce the handicrafts that are on display at high prices in the stores.

But at irregular intervals along its straight course are found individuals of apparently even greater deprivation than the industrious Neapolitan poor. On the pavement, sitting or lying, the homeless and the penniless, the crippled and the forgotten present pitiful tales or pleas on scraps of card. A begging hippy and ragged gypsy children pour colour upon colour under the triumphant sun embracing all as equal: the sea, Vesuvio and another day.

A Question of Class

La Dolce Vita

3   The Neapolitan fisherman asleep in the afternoon sun was approached by a well-to-do businessman from another city. 'Why are you asleep instead of doing something useful?' 'What should I do?' answered the fisherman. 'You could mend your nets,' suggested the businessman, 'and then you would catch more fish. If you caught more fish you would make more money and sooner or later you could afford a bigger fishing boat which would enable you to catch still more fish. In time you could become the owner of several boats and employ other fishermen to work for you. Eventually you would become a wealthy man with a fleet of fishing boats bringing ashore great quantities of fish and earning more than enough money for you and your family to live in great style. You would no longer need to work hard or worry about the future. In fact, you'd have la dolce vita. Come on! Wake up! The day is short but there's still time to attain your ambitions.'

The fisherman listened patiently – he had enjoyed a long lunch and felt quite drowsy in the warm afternoon sun – and when the man was finished looked at him puzzled. 'I would do all that to have la dolce vita? Why should I do all that to achieve what I already have?'

Manchester Today

4   A recent report on the present-day social conditions in Manchester draws attention to the following statistics

* More than one in three Mancunians rely on social security
* 20,000 houses are affected by damp
* 30,000 homes lack essential heating
* The death rate is 65% above the normal national average

Questions

a) Explain the difference in attitude between Engels and his acquaintance in text 1.
b) What is meant by the phrase *conspicuous consumption* in text 2?
c) What is the great equaliser in Naples according to text 2?
d) What is the moral of the story about the fisherman in text 3? Say why you agree or disagree with the point of view of the businessman.
e) How would you describe the conditions many Mancunians live in today according to text 4?
f) Discuss the proposition that there will always be rich and poor in any society, referring to the examples above.

Now turn to the grammar exercises on page 77.

Listening

During a visit to London, a European tourist is discussing British newspapers with an English acquaintance over a pub lunch. Listen to the tape and make notes on the papers and their readership according to the conversation. Try and identify the social categories referred to in relation to the newspapers and suggest some occupations for each of these categories.

Class in Europe – a historical perspective

The following extract is taken from *The Pelican History of the World* by J.M. Roberts.

The rise of the merchant class was intimately linked with the growth of towns and trade; that is to say that they were linked with the most dynamic element in medieval European civilisation and one hostile to its feudal setting. It was an element which not only produced new wealth but new institutions. Feudal institutions did not work easily in a society of tradesmen and craftsmen for which they had no adequate theoretical place. Yet feudal lords sought the support of towns against kings and kings sought the support of townsmen and their wealth against overmighty subjects. They gave towns charters and privileges. The walls which surrounded the medieval city were often the symbol and guarantee of its immunity. 'The air of a town makes you free' said a German proverb. The communes and within them the guilds were associations of free men for a long time isolated in a world unfree. The burgher – the bourgeois, the dweller in bourg or borough – was a man who stood up for himself in a universe of dependence.

This salient characteristic of the new middle class is echoed today by the British Prime Minister, Margaret Thatcher, when she refers to the danger posed by a 'nanny state' in its propensity to encourage dependency among the population.

a) What new institutions do you think were produced by the rise of the merchants?
b) Provide another word meaning *dweller*.
c) What is a *bourg* or *borough*?
d) Explain the phrase *stood up for himself*.
e) What is meant by a *nanny state*?
f) How does the class structure of Britain compare with social stratification in your own country?

Language Activity

Read the following notes which describe the formal debating procedure and prepare to debate the motion below.

Four main speakers are required: a proposer and seconder for the motion and an opposing speaker and seconder against the motion. These four prepare their speeches and use notes to help them as they speak. The aim is to be as clear and persuasive as possible.

A 'chair' (person who runs or controls a debate) should also be appointed. Speeches are in this order: main speaker for the motion, main speaker against the motion, seconder for, seconder against. The role of the chair is to introduce the debate and the individual speakers. After the main speeches the chair throws the debate open to the 'floor' (the rest of the class). Then the main speakers sum up their arguments with the opposer going first and the vote is taken on the motion. The chair announces the result by saying that the motion is carried, or defeated and by how many.

'This house believes that in the late twentieth century the concept of class is no longer relevant.'

Media Watch

* Take any two European countries and make a list of major national daily papers. Find out what social and political profiles the papers present and decide whether political connections are overt or covert.

* From a study of either TV commercials or cinema, describe the role of class in advertising in any European country. Identify products that are connected with certain social groups and put your findings into list form.

A Romantic Vision

The following poem by William Wordsworth called *The Solitary Reaper*, which was written in 1803, depicts an individual from a particular class as viewed from the (romantic) perspective of another class.

> Behold her, single in the field,
> Yon solitary Highland Lass!
> Reaping and singing by herself;
> Stop here, or gently pass!
> Alone she cuts and binds the grain,
> And sings a melancholy strain;
> O listen! for the vale profound
> Is overflowing with the sound.

Describe the subject of the poem in realistic terms.

Afterthoughts

In people's China the workers take the lead. In Capitalist Britain the beggars also take the copper, iron, floorboards + fillings from your teeth!

Joke! A man goes to see a psychiatrist and complains, 'Doctor, I'm afraid I have an inferiority complex'.

After some consideration the psychiatrist replies, 'Please don't worry about it any more – you are inferior'.

Housewives' Choice?

"If the gentler sex is now 45% of the workforce—"

"—why the Hell do we only earn 28% of employment income!"

Evans

unit two

On average, women in the UK earn two-thirds of the average man's salary. Why?

Man with his superior physical strength can better undertake the more strenuous tasks... not handicapped, as is woman, by the physiological burdens of pregnancy and nursing.

from *Social Structure* by George P. Murdock 1965

Read the text and as you do so consider the following questions. Remember, you don't have to understand every word in order to answer them.

1 In what ways has the position of working women improved?

2 Which jobs are women more likely to do in comparison with men?

A Woman's Place

It is only sixty years since British women gained the right to vote in parliamentary elections. Some people think this is the main reason women are so under-represented in politics, trades unions and big business. Others feel it is simply that they are much too busy doing other things. The old phrase, 'a woman's place is in the home' may seem out of date to most people, but the stereotyped image of woman as supporting wife and nurturing mother is certainly still commonplace – one only has to watch a few television commercials.

In 1975 the Equal Pay Act made it, theoretically, illegal for women to be paid less than men for doing the same work. Certainly it is usually the case nowadays that women doing the same jobs as men get the same money for doing it; but generally women do not do the same jobs: they do different ones that attract lower salaries. The areas women work in are still overwhelmingly those of 'service'; teaching, nursing, catering and cleaning, jobs that can be seen as an extension of the mothering role. Even top secretaries, we are told, are prepared to make the tea for their predominantly male bosses, despite the fact that their administrative and technical skills have taken years to perfect.

Apart from looking after people during the day at work, women often have to take care of a family at home too, which may mean they have less energy to compete in the rat race for career development. In almost every field management positions are more likely to be filled by men. While the majority of teachers are women, for example, the majority of headteachers are not. There are many female doctors entering the profession today but the woman consultant is still a rarity. School cooks are female, top chefs are men and even cleaners tend to be supervised by male caretakers.

Sometimes when a job becomes associated with women the status and corollaries, such as remuneration, decline. A hundred years ago a 'private secretary', who would be male, had far higher status than the average female secretary of today who is not always recognised as being a professional at all and rarely paid as such. If the mere presence of females in a profession diminishes the respect in which it is held it is easy to see that the feminist movement still has an important campaigning role to play; there is still a long way to travel down the road to Equal Opportunities.

Comprehension

1 In what areas are women said to be under-represented?

2 Do the majority of people agree that 'a woman's place is in the home'?

3 How are women often depicted in advertisements?

4 What was the purpose of the Equal Pay Act?

5 Why do women earn less than men fifteen years after the Act?
6 Give examples from the text of female-dominated occupations.
7 In what ways are teachers and secretaries like mothers?
8 Give a possible reason why female employees fail to reach high positions in their area of work.
9 Find a word or phrase in the text that means

old-fashioned	over-generalisation
against the law	oversee or direct
take care of	competition for promotion
pay (noun)	important job

Think of another word or phrase for

status	looking after
campaigning	corollaries
value	diminishes
apart from	feminist

10 Find antonyms (opposites) of the following from the text

minority	husband
in practice	legal
seldom	under-represented

The Biological Argument

1 Many of our attitudes about female employment seem to come almost directly from the nineteenth century when the exciting new science of anthropology (the study of humankind), served, to some extent, to reinforce prejudices about a woman's place. The following passage by Murdock illustrates this. He argues that gender-based division of labour is natural and universal. When do you imagine the following was written? (answer on the first page of this unit).

Man with his superior physical strength can better undertake the more strenuous tasks, such as lumbering, mining, quarrying, land clearance and housebuilding. Not handicapped, as is woman, by the physiological burdens of pregnancy and nursing, he can range farther afield to hunt, to fish, to herd and to trade. Woman is at no disadvantage, however, in lighter tasks which can be performed in or near the home, eg the gathering of vegetable products, the fetching of water, the preparation of food and the manufacture of clothing and utensils. All known human societies have developed specialisation and co-operation between the sexes roughly along this biologically determined line of cleavage...

The advantages inherent in a division of labour by sex presumably account for its universality... The man, perhaps returns from a day of hunting, chilled, unsuccessful and with his clothing soiled and torn, to find warmth before a fire which he could not have maintained, to eat food gathered and cooked by the woman instead of going hungry and to receive fresh garments for the morrow, prepared, mended or laundered by her hands. Or perhaps the woman has found no vegetable food... the man in his ramblings after game can readily supply her wants.

Housewives' Choice? *Interpretations in English*

Consider the following

* Do people of all cultures divide work in a similar fashion?
* Do you think pregnancy is a handicap?
* Are wood, water and vegetable gathering light jobs?
* Is modern day housework light work?

The Socialist Situation

2 It is, perhaps, surprising to discover that in the Soviet Union women still earn less than their male comrades. As in Europe, they do different jobs that attract lower salaries. Look at the table below. Pick out the occupations which are male dominated in Western countries including your own. What kind of pay do these jobs attract when done by men? Are you surprised by any of the statistics?

The following list of women's professions was compiled in the Soviet Union in 1970. The picture has not changed appreciably since then.

Profession	Percentage of Women
Nurses	99
Typists	99
Day-care personnel	98
Pediatricians	98
Secretaries	95
Librarians	95
Cashiers	94
Clothing industry	88
Laboratory personnel	85
Midwives	83
Telephone operators	83
Managerial personnel in institutions	82
Computer operators	77
Doctors	74
Workers in food industries	74
Teachers	72
Textile workers	72

These professions are among the lowest paid. A teacher, for example, makes 100 roubles a month as a starting salary and 145 roubles after long service; a miner usually makes more than 200 roubles. A 1972 budget proposed for the Soviet working family assumed that the man's salary was fifty per cent higher than the woman's – it was taken for granted that the woman worked and she was badly paid.

from *Moscow Women* by Carola Hansson and Karin Liden

* Are you surprised by these statistics?

Interpretations in English   Housewives' Choice?

An Italian Perspective

3   Tourists in Rome were surprised to see a woman driving a huge orange tractor down Rome's via del Tritone.

Italy's political leaders and some of its male union chiefs are said to have been even more surprised to see that the tractor was followed by an estimated 200,000 women in an unprecedented procession that took more than three hours to snake through central Rome.

Chanting slogans, waving flags and dancing to drumbeats, the women had come to the capital from all over Italy to demonstrate for a 'a job for each of us, a different type of job and a society without violence'.

Political support is growing for a national law promoting widespread action that would remove the continued obstacles to greater employment and advancement for women and provide incentives for women seeking to start in business.

Feminists like Ms Palleschi charge that slavish dedication and other male attitudes to work are not necessarily to be held up as a model. 'Furthermore, if the law removed many forms of formal discrimination, it has not removed the latent discrimination that continues to block women's advancement,' says Isfol's Michou Cattan.

from an article in the *Financial Times* 18th April 1988

Discussion Point

* How far should the nature of work be changed, as Palleschi suggests, in order to attract more women into the ranks of the employed?

Now turn to the grammar exercises on page 78.

Listening

Listen carefully to the radio broadcast in which you will hear a debate on the role of women and answer the following questions.

1. What alternative phrases are suggested for 'housewife'?
2. What is the title of Anne Morris' new book?
3. Explain Baroness Hawkes' phrase 'the fruits of your labour'.
4. Explain the problems of women factory workers.
5. Why do some children turn to crime and drugs according to Baroness Hawkes?
6. In what sense is a housewife 'unrewarded' according to Anne Morris?

* Now summarise in writing the positions taken by the two women. Try to express each point of view in 60 to 70 words.

* In her introduction Jenny Parkes counterpoises two views of what it means to be a housewife. Are they mutually exclusive?

unit two

Housewives' Choice?   Interpretations in English

Media Watch

A   Look at the advertisement below for two novels. Work in groups.

a) Who do you think the advertisement is aimed at?

b) From reading the text of the advert, can you say anything about the roles of the main protagonists? (eg active/passive, high status/low status etc)

c) What adjectives are used to describe them?

d) List the similarities and differences between the two books and their leading characters.

e) Explain why the titles might be attractive to the intended readership.

f) Divide into small groups and discuss how the plots of the books might develop and, together, work on a brief storyline for one of them.

EXPERIENCE THE MYSTERY AND MAGIC OF THE EAST WITH TWO COMPELLING NEW SAGAS

JOHN MACCABEE

Lustre

Impetuous Tom Aspinall abandons the glitz of New York society to become a South Seas' pearl trader – and becomes rich beyond his wildest dreams

But an old rival relentlessly tracks him down, to destroy everything Tom has built and everyone Tom loves.

STEPHANIE *AND JADE*

BOTH OUT NOW IN PAPERBACK

---

14   unit two

Interpretations in English — **Housewives' Choice?**

B Advertising makes use of many stereotypes, particularly to do with the roles of men and women. Watch out for advertisements and TV commercials, either in English or your own language, that deal with male and female images. Make notes in the spaces provided on the roles people play using the example to help you. Try and complete five more.

Discuss in advance what might be meant by

* status (high or low)
* active/passive behaviour
* *young and beautiful* stereotype
* *motherly* stereotype

It will also be interesting to note whether women and men are seen outdoors or indoors and with what objects/instruments etc they are associated.

Product	Martini	Product	
woman	high status, passive, indoors with glass, mostly listening, young and beautiful		
man	high status, active, outdoors, with glass and yacht		

Product		Product	

Product		Product	

unit two

C

Language is very important in its power to present and define images of ourselves and others. For example, certain terms of address convey more than one level of meaning. In England sometimes affectionate terms of endearment when used to address a stranger can suggest an assumed superiority over the addressee. The passage below explains this phenomenon more fully.

Words don't just carry meaning like containers. Meaning is not constant: it is negotiated in the context of interaction among people. Terms of address, terms of endearment, and pronouns like *tu* and *vous* in French can be put to work in conversations to convey many different meanings. A term of endearment like *luv* can be used by both women and men to express intimacy or solidarity; or it can be used as a putdown. Most women can remember occasions when they have been attempting to make a serious point in a conversation or in a meeting at work and their conversation has been dismissed by a man in terms such as: *Oh, come on, luv*; or, *Don't worry, sunshine*.

from a letter published in *The Guardian* 25th November 1987

Explain the following

solidarity   *terms of endearment*
a putdown   *negotiated*

* Have you come across any other examples of terms of endearment being used in this way?

Questionnaire

Look at the questionnaire on the next page.

Find out who does what among your friends and relations (or host family). Put one, two or no ticks for each job. Ask male and female respondents separately. List the jobs that are done by one person only and the shared jobs. Compare your results with other members of the class. Are there marked differences in the case of

older women
single (divorced etc)
professional women
non-British women

Example Questions

* Who washes the car, you or your husband?
* Who does the ironing, you or your girlfriend?

Interpretations in English — **Housewives' Choice?**

JOB	Done by woman	Done by man
wash the car		
clean toilet		
wire plugs		
empty dustbins		
sewing		
ironing		
hand washing		
machine washing		
weeding		
decorating		
food shopping		
clothes shopping		
mow the lawn		
put up shelves		
feed the pets		
vacuuming		
dusting		
pay the bills		
organise child care		
change car tyre		
drive the car		
Brief description of woman (status, age, profession etc)		

Facts and Figures

The following statistics are taken from government figures on male and female wage levels in 1988.

Percentage	men	women
10% earn less than	£127	£92
25% earn less than	£162	£112
50% earn less than	£215	£145
25% earn more than	£288	£198
10% earn more than	£384	£258

The average weekly wage in April 1988 for a woman was £164. The average weekly wage for men was £246.

Comment on the above figures.

Afterthought

The Queen is most anxious to enlist every one who can speak or write to join in checking this mad, wicked folly of 'Woman's Rights', with all its attendant horrors, on which her poor feeble sex is bent, forgetting every sense of womanly feeling and propriety. It is a subject which makes the Queen so furious that she cannot contain herself. God created men and women different; then let them remain each in their own position.

Letter to Sir Theodore Martin, 29th May 1870 from Queen Victoria.

'The battle for women's rights has largely been won.'
Margaret Thatcher 1982

The Fourth Estate

unit three

The Fourth Estate

Only an informed public can prevent the undermining of democracy and freedom.

This observation underlines the importance to a democracy of having available a wide range of accurate information from many different sources and viewpoints.

Read the text and as you do so consider the following questions. Remember, you don't have to understand every word in order to answer them.

1. What are the new press 'freedoms'?
2. Who suffers from them?

Paper Tigers

'Mr Harris has asked us to point out a number of inaccuracies in our story. After returning from India he served in Ireland for four years and not six months as stated; he has never farmed at Heddington, particularly not at Coate Road Farm as stated; he has never counted cycling or walking among his hobbies; he is not a member of 54 hunts; and he did not have an eye removed at Chippenham hospital after an air raid.' This is not a real correction, but a fictional one which appears in Howard Brenton and David Hare's Fleet Street satire, *Pravda*.

Real corrections are few and far between in the British press and they're never as long as that. It seems incredible but there is no legal obligation on them to correct their mistakes. Politicians have traditionally been loathe to tamper with the much-vaunted Freedom of the Press. But the behaviour of certain elements of the British press in recent months have led some people to point out that this freedom should not lead to distortion of the facts, let alone deliberate libel and the invasion of people's privacy. Most to blame are *The Sun* and the *News of the World*, circulation four million and five million respectively and both owned by Rupert Murdoch's News International. NI also owns *The Times* of London and newspapers and television stations in North America and Australia.

Standing against this modern tide of misinformation is the Press Council, a body which can impose no punishment, cannot call witnesses and bases its rulings on no fixed code of principles. It wields only moral authority, a puny weapon against a powerful industry where morality is more often preached about than practised and which has never been keen to admit its errors. In 1986 the Press Council upheld four complaints against *The Sun*; the following year it upheld fifteen. Successful complaints against the *News of the World* went up from three to eight in the same period.

Supporters of the two papers frequently point to their huge circulation figures as vindication of their editorial policies. It certainly seems true that their readers care little for the truth or otherwise of what they read at their breakfast tables. So it is being left to the large corporate advertisers such as Boots and Sainsbury and Dixon, all jealous of their clean family image, to blow the whistle. They have the economic muscle to restrain reporting excesses and now seem prepared to withdraw their patronage if journalists refuse to clean up their act. In the meantime the Mr Harrises of this world must try not to fall foul of the press and its freedoms.

Interpretations in English   The Fourth Estate

Glossary

few and far between	infrequent
loathe to	unwilling to
much-vaunted	often boasted about
blow the whistle	draw attention, especially in order to stop (something)
the Mr Harrises of this world	people such as Mr Harris
fall foul of	make an enemy of

Comprehension

1. Explain the irony in the phrase *a number of inaccuracies*.
2. Where and what is Fleet Street?
3. Why do newspapers rarely print corrections or apologies?
4. Why do you think the concept of press freedom is considered to be so important?
5. In what ways has this traditional 'freedom' been abused by some editors of major newspapers?
6. Why do some papers deliberately print inaccurate material?
7. Explain the term *circulation* in this context.
8. What do you understand to be the function of the Press Council?
9. Why is it ineffective?
10. How is it companies such as Boots have
    a) the power, and
    b) the desire to restrain the excesses of certain papers?

Test Cases

1

The row over the reporting of the British army's shooting of three IRA bombers in Gibraltar in April showed the British media at its worst. Thames Television was quite entitled to question eyewitnesses in order to reconstruct the events. And Thames had every right to expect that British newspapers would support its action. But in the event the Prime Minister's outrage was supported by many elements of the press, which not only attacked the programme-makers' treatment of the story, but also immediately set about libelling those who appeared in the programme in order to question their credibility.

The one exception was *The Observer*, which followed up the TV programme with its own investigations into what might really have happened in Gibraltar. *The Sunday Times* was content to follow the government line, with the headline 'Gibraltar killings row: SAS will be vindicated' while the *Sunday Telegragh* headlined its piece: 'Gibraltar film flawed, says expert witness'; all of which recalls the press reaction to the killings themselves, which was to print without independent verification the government's reports of a massive car bomb and remote triggering devices, both of which turned out to be false.

unit three

The Fourth Estate *Interpretations in English*

Fleet Street's <u>pro-government bias</u> has always existed, but its feverish desire to back Margaret Thatcher in everything she does is now leading it to support her in actions where Fleet Street itself could be the ultimate victim. For <u>the fetters</u> with which Mrs Thatcher is now trying to restrict television reporters could equally <u>ensnare</u> the ankles of newspaper journalists.

* What was the 'row' about?

* Explain the positions of
  a) The Prime Minister
  b) Thames TV
  c) British newspapers

2 The Prime Minister has warned the media to help identify members of the mob which murdered two soldiers at an IRA funeral in West Belfast in March. If they fail to comply, they will stand accused of siding with terrorism.

Mrs Thatcher's words in the House highlighted the confrontation over the refusal of the broadcasting authorities to hand over film of the mob attack without a court order. She was strongly supported by Tory backbenchers, one of whom had already declared that the media was 'not above the law'. Mrs Thatcher said: 'I believe everyone, the media included, has a bounden duty to do everything they can to see that those who perpetrated the terrible crime we saw on television, and which disgusted the whole world, are brought to justice.' Her supporters cheered as she continued: 'Either one is on the side of justice in these matters or one is on the side of terrorism.'

Journalists have already made clear the dangers they face if they are seen to be agents of the security services. One spokesperson said: 'If we hand our film over, then no journalist will be safe to work in Northern Ireland again. And that could lead to a news blackout in the province.'

* Why were journalists unwilling to surrender film of an IRA funeral?

* Comment on the phrase 'Either one is on the side of justice... or of terrorism.'

3 A disturbing picture faced *Sunday Telegraph* readers last Sunday: it showed the body of one of the soldiers killed the previous day in West Belfast, lying arms akimbo with a priest kneeling nearby. According to the paper's editor, the picture '...conveyed the truth of the event more accurately than any words. The picture', he added, 'had a Christ-like quality, like the crucifixion.'

Many of his readers felt differently and have been writing and phoning in to complain about what they thought was a gratuitously offensive photograph. The paper had apparently bought it for two hundred pounds from an unnamed source. On the Monday, *Today* published a similar picture of the body, but in full colour, on the front page. There were five more pictures inside. Like the *Sunday Telegraph*, *Today* has received numerous complaints.

The Press Council frequently investigates allegations of bad taste, when it has to determine in effect, whether a particular item is published because it is genuinely newsworthy, or whether it's there just to boost circulation. In 1986 complaints against a Glasgow newspaper's picture of a child

unit three

Interpretations in English — **The Fourth Estate**

slipping out of a fireman's grasp during a fire at a high-level tenement were rejected because there was, at the time, a campaign to prevent fires in tenement blocks. Last year, an *Evening Standard* photograph of a man jumping to his death was allowed because the suicide had planned his fall as an act of public protest. However, it is expected that *The Sun* will be censured for a recent photograph of a two-headed baby, currently under investigation by the Press Council.

* Discuss what moral issues are involved in the publication of the photograph of the dead soldier in Northern Ireland. Have you seen 'gratuitously offensive' material in your daily/weekly newspaper?

Vocabulary

There are certain English words which, when used in connection with journalism, take on specialist meanings. Here are some examples

hack	reporter (from hackney carriage or taxi, the route of which covers the same old ground every day)
hackneyed phrase	cliché
story	article (the material is supposedly factual, though some papers do indeed deal in fictitious 'stories')
circulation	number of copies sold (nowadays papers do not 'circulate' round many readers)
copy	material written for publication, often measured in 'column inches'
tabloid	small format newspaper (the term once meant a chemical concentration, and these papers certainly are easier to handle and to read, but the tabloid form is now strongly associated with the gutter press – popular, down-market titles)

Now turn to the grammar exercises on page 79.

Listening

The recorded conversation is between the editor, assistant editor, news editor and advertising sales manager of a typical British newspaper. Listen to the tape and answer the questions.

1. What is the first front page headline the editor considers?
2. Why is Lord Whatsisname's sex life newsworthy?
3. Who appears to have been the main informant for the article?
4. Why might the Press Council object to the 'vice story'?
5. What do you understand by the expression *paper tiger*?
6. How does the news editor justify the inclusion of the article?
7. What offences did the politician's wife commit?
8. Why are a number of reporters and photographers waiting at a Manchester hospital?
9. What information is the assistant editor hoping for from the West Indian hotel porter?
10. Why did the peer sue the paper after a recent 'supernatural' story?

Discussion Points

In groups, discuss the following questions. Make a note of the main points of view to report back to the class.

* Are stories about the lives of royalty and entertainers suitable for the front page?
* Do you enjoy reading 'gossip' items in your daily/weekly newspaper? Do you believe they are true?
* Should there be a law against the invasion of privacy? Explain the situation in your own country.

Language Activity

Imagine your group is the Press Council. Write down any objections you have about the articles suggested by the team in the recorded dialogue. Prepare to argue your case.

Media Watch

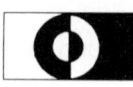

Collect examples of *The Sun* and *News of the World* (Sundays only) in Britain or of similar newspapers and magazines from your own country.

Make a note of

a) 'Royals' stories

b) 'Vice' stories

c) 'Soap' stories (articles about actors who are familiar from TV serials or 'soap operas'. Often the character's name is used instead of the actor's own name and there is a blurring of reality and fiction.)

d) Serious news articles

* Try to decide the rough percentage of 'real' news in each paper or magazine. Compare your estimate with other members of your class.

* Collect examples of serious newspapers and see if there is a much greater percentage of 'real' news in these.

* Collect examples of some of the more outlandish papers, for example *The Sunday Sport*. Make notes on the editorial policies of these papers, eg with regard to invasion of privacy, taste, accuracy, libel etc. Notice what stories are chosen to lead, and what headlines and captions are used.

Afterthought

In early 1989, Rupert Murdoch's News International Group gained control of the book publishers William Collins. The Collins board had recommended that shareholders should accept the bid. Faced with the choice of ending a long and successful relationship with their publisher or contributing to the profits of a powerful and influential media empire which they may have regarded as right-wing, many authors are in an unenviable predicament.

Television is Watching You!

unit four

Television is Watching You!   Interpretations in English

Fact!

On an average day in 1977, Venezuelans heard or read 100 news items from the USA for every seven stories sent the other way round; and these seven were all sent via AP or UPI – both US news agencies.

By his or her sixteenth birthday, the average child in the USA has watched 50,000 murders or attempted murders and about 200,000 acts of violence – all on television.

Read the text and as you do so consider the following questions. Remember, you don't have to understand every word in order to answer them.

1. Why is the advent of satellite television more important than, say, that of home videos?
2. Who is going to benefit from DBS?

News from Space

European broadcasting is undergoing a revolution called Direct Broadcast by Satellite. Satellites broadcasting down to master antennae for re-broadcast to domestic TV sets is old hat. The new DBS apparatus is powerful enough to beam down direct to the viewer via smaller dishes on his or her roof. Four entrepreneurs are poised to make the most of the new DBS opportunities: Robert Maxwell (who owns *The Daily Mirror* and publishing and print companies in the UK), Rupert Murdoch (owner of News International and media interests in many countries), American Ted Turner and Silvio Berlusconi.

Satellite broadcasting has aroused some serious misgivings throughout the world. With three satellites theoretically capable of transmitting to the whole globe, many people fear that weaker countries may be trodden down by the 'footprint' of a wealthy neighbour's satellite. Third World countries also fear that, if and when they can afford their own satellites, all the best sites for them and all the best frequencies may already have been snapped up. Rich countries are already beginning to exploit their technical advantage. For example, the US uses satellite to transmit its daily two-hour programme *America Today*. Its mix of arts and sport is available free and not unnaturally, is used up by cable operators and national broadcasting systems throughout the world, including the BBC and ITV in the United Kingdom.

US embassies in many countries are now equipped with satellite dishes. When US government officials wish to speak to foreign journalists, these can be invited to attend 'interactive press conferences' at the local embassy, while the government officials broadcast from their own offices in Washington. In one of the first such conferences, Jean Kirkpatrick, US ambassador to the United Nations, explained why her country decided to invade the Caribbean island of Grenada in October 1983. Henry Kissinger was said to be '...enthusiastic about this dramatic new device to reach people abroad'.

Along with certain dubious political implications, DBS may also, in the long run, threaten the quality of TV which is available to the ordinary consumer. When programme makers have the whole world as their market, won't they be under pressure to produce bland and unexceptional programmes to appeal to the largest audiences, ignoring minority or ethnic interests? And won't the poorer countries be tempted to buy cheaply or accept for nothing the offerings of their richer neighbours at the expense of their own developing broadcasting industries? Perhaps the most sobering thought of all is that, given the power of the new satellites, individual governments will be powerless to prevent the importation of 'wall-to-wall Dallas' into their countries.

unit four

Interpretations in English | Television is Watching You!

Glossary
- **old hat** — nothing new
- **snap up** — take, grab, quickly or immediately
- **globe** — world
- **wall-to-wall** — the same pattern everywhere (usually of carpets)

Comprehension

1. What is the difference between the old-style satellites and the new DBS?
2. What exactly is an *entrepreneur*?
3. Why are some countries unhappy about the innovation of DBS?
4. In what sense is the satellite broadcast of *America Today* an exploitation of the USA's 'technical advantage'?
5. What do you understand by the term *interactive press conference*?
6. What kind of programme is feared to be likely to predominate with the spread of DBS?
7. What kind of programmes will be less likely to be made?
8. How are Third World broadcasting industries threatened by cheap foreign programmes?
9. Explain the phrase *wall-to-wall Dallas*.
10. Find synonyms in the text for the first column of words and antonyms for the second

equipment	trivial
locations	stronger
as well as	without flavour
poor	enthusiastic

Satellite Broadcasting and British TV

[handwritten: 2 organisations administer British TV – who are they?]

1 *Will British TV monopolies withstand the DBS threat?*

British television is administered by two organisations which are technically independent of the government: the British Broadcasting Corporation and the Independent Broadcasting Authority. The BBC also administers four national radio services, many local radio stations and the External Services which include the English language World Service and the foreign language sections. In addition to independent television, the IBA also administers 46 independent local radio stations. *(Name 2)*

ITV is a commercial network and is made up of fifteen regional channels such as Thames and London Weekend Television in London, Harlech in Wales and Granada in the North West. Other organisations beneath the IBA umbrella are Channel Four, Independent Television News and TV-AM, the early morning channel. BBC1 and BBC2 do not accept advertising but are funded by an annual license fee which all viewers must pay and is fixed by the government. As a general rule, Channel Four and BBC2 cater more for minority tastes and interests while BBC1 and ITV aim for larger audiences and broadcast, by and large, more commercial material.

unit four

The BBC and IBA have jealously guarded their broadcasting monopolies, stamping out independent radio broadcasters known as pirate radio stations, wherever these have appeared. Satellite broadcasting now threatens their monopoly in television and, partly in order to turn the industry into a leaner fitter animal, the Conservative government is also intent on undermining this monopoly. The possibility of ending the existence of *public service broadcasting* is being contemplated and many voices call for advertising to contribute to the funding of all television production.

* What do you understand by the term *public service broadcasting*?

* Explain briefly the structure of television in the Britain of the late eighties.

2 The government's proposals for breaking up the monopoly positions of the BBC and IBA in television to allow greater competition will inevitably mean that production costs will become a more significant factor within the industry. Budgets will be tighter. The movement towards curtailing the monopoly also brings with it an increase in the importance of advertising. The large TV organisations are to be sold off to the highest bidders. In short, unfettered competition will govern the media industry just as it does washing powders in the supermarket. The number of viewers will be equivalent to the number of packets sold.

Like circulation figures of a newspaper, ratings figures will be waved at advertisers in an attempt to demand high rates and thereby maintain profits. Popularity and not controversy will be the name of the game and a wealth of expertise and creativity will be devoted to this single aim.

* Explain the phrases *sold off to the highest bidders* and *unfettered competition*.

* According to the passage, what is likely to happen after the break-up of monopoly television?

3 If advertisers call the tune will programmes become more popular? The question to be addressed is, will advertisers behave similarly and demand high ratings per se or will some, at least, be content with more moderate figures provided they are targeting a specific sector of the audience? Should advertisers have such influence over the output of television anyway, regardless of the consequences?

One argument advanced is that with the increasing fragmentation of markets into more and more minority groups, such as teenagers, young professionals, working class mothers, well-to-do retired people etc, advertisers will be looking for minority interest programmes that will be watched by limited numbers of people but, largely, just the very people that the advertiser wants to reach. Television would then be able to charge the kind of rates that quality programming depends on. If this scenario proves accurate then programmes such as those presently screened by BBC2 and Channel Four would proliferate under the new conditions.

If this is not the case, and programmes in general become more popularist, will this necessarily lead to the production of either programmes of poor quality or of bland and trivial character? Will entertainment of the lowest common denominator prevail? Will they be predominantly American soap operas, cheap games shows and uncontroversial sanitised news features concentrating on sensational and popularist output in both form and content? Or will there really be greater freedom of choice and a wider range of programmes to suit all tastes?

* What is meant by the expression *the lowest common denominator*?
* Explain the difference between rates and ratings.
* What does the writer suggest could be the positive results of the re-organisation of television in the UK?

4   *Will TV – and the media in general – soon exercise political control over the population of the world?*

As more countries develop their economies and begin to participate in the international economy the number of people who have access to television grows. It is clear, then, that only those who underestimate the influence of television can remain unperturbed by the concentration of media power into a few hands. To those in doubt, if TV did not have great power to affect people's thoughts and actions then why does America beam ideological broadcasts towards its perceived enemies and why did the Soviet Union before Gorbachev go to great lengths to jam them? Surely, all media output is propaganda of a kind and as such will arouse strong support and strong opposition.

Notwithstanding blatant propaganda, values are always implicit in any piece of film or video because each broadcast piece has been carefully written, edited, directed and produced by individuals and groups in specific socio-political contexts. They are very likely to have quite strong and well defined, implicit or explicit, political and moral positions. In addition to this, satellites launched into space under the pretext of providing news and entertainment services often end up being used for military purposes.

Does anybody have the right to smuggle into foreign countries great quantities of mind-bending substances? Satellite broadcasting can avoid customs procedures. Is this the meaning of freedom of expression? Surely freedom should exist between equals? Is there any kind of balance between the number of American programmes watched by citizens in Eastern Europe and the quantity of programmes of the Soviet Union or Third World countries seen by those in the West?

* Explain what is meant by the following

underestimate	*unperturbed*	*blatant propaganda*
ideological	*values*	*socio-political contexts*
smuggle	*avoid*	*mind-bending substances*

* In the light of experience from other European countries what might you expect to happen after the advent of unlimited competition in Britain and will this be good or bad?

Now turn to the grammar exercises on page 80.

Did you realize that over 3/4 of the information absorbed by the public comes from the television?

That's terrible, I don't believe it! Where on earth did you hear that?

I think it was on 'Media Watch' last Friday.

Television is Watching You!   *Interpretations in English*

Listening

The recorded discussion is based on a television programme about the future shape of current affairs in TV in the light of government censorship, pressure to compete for advertising and the threat from satellite broadcasting.

At the heart of the discussion is the concept of *infotainment* – a new form of current affairs, based on American formats, that relies on feature journalism. This child of our times argues that conventional current affairs will only be watched if injected with a strong dose of show business techniques. It doesn't show what's going on in the world. Infotainment is entertaining but notable for what it will not tackle: few investigations into political or commercial corruption and a propensity to take the easy option.

Speaker A is an editor of current affairs and news programmes. Speaker B is a producer of an 'infotainment' type current affairs programme. Speaker C chairs the discussion. Speaker A begins by defending traditional investigative current affairs against the charge that it is somehow a protected species and unconcerned about popular appeal.

Study the glossary below before listening to the tape and making notes on the arguments put forward by A and B. Summarise their opinions on 'infotainment'.

Glossary

Sainsbury's	the name of a large chain of supermarkets
vested interests	people or companies that have a share in something to their advantage which they want to protect
pincer movement	attack from two sides
ratings	the number of people who have watched a particular television programme based on sampling and statistics
popular slots	peak viewing times
muzzling	silencing (preventing from expressing opinion)
auctioning	selling something to the highest bidder
franchise	the right to offer a product or service under an established name
throw overboard	to dispose of

Questionnaire

Do a survey and find out which kind of television people enjoy. Ask for three choices in order of preference. Use some of the example programme types listed below and fill in the table opposite.

western	horror film	news and current affairs
documentaries	music	sport
soap operas	thrillers	games shows
plays	chat shows	historical drama
variety shows	natural history	cookery
politics	comedy	science fiction films

30   *unit four*

Fill in the chart below entering information regarding programme types and category of interviewee (age, sex, occupation etc).

| Interviewee ||| Programme Categories |
Age	Sex	Occupation	

Media Watch

A In groups, find copies of publications that include detailed descriptions of TV and radio programmes. Use the television page information from an edition of *The Guardian* newspaper as a starting point and compare programmes on the different channels. Choose two or three programmes or the day's schedule from each channel and explain how they represent the character of the channel.

B Try and assess the influence of American programmes by working out the number of such programmes as a proportion of the total. Base your results on a week's viewing.

Language Activity

Until recently, television was silent on Thursdays in Iceland to allow families time to talk. Prepare to argue the case for a TV free day in your country, including all the possible benefits.

Afterthought

It has been shown that the most enriching and joyful forms of human activity are either social or include physical exercise. Television fails on both counts.

Soft Sell

unit five

A new trend in advertising is the tease – not the sexual tease – but the tease which, as often as not leaves the consumer wondering: 'What on earth are they selling?'

Read the text and as you do so consider the following questions. Remember, you don't have to understand every word in order to answer them.

1. What kind of advertising is the most popular today?
2. Are there any restrictions on what advertisers can do?

The Soft Sell

A recent billboard campaign for a new board game cost the manufacturers over £100,000, but left the man and woman in the street no wiser. The game was called 'UBI', which means 'where' in Latin. The advertising agency thought up the clever message 'Where is UBI?' The manufacturing company was inundated with calls from car drivers whose car registration included the letters UBI; they all thought they had won a prize. A television advertising campaign for a chocolate bar also had the consumers thinking: 'Great ad, but what is the product?' They phoned the TV station in their thousands to ask when the new TV series was going to be broadcast. When the penny finally dropped that WISPA was a type of confectionery and not a spy thriller, it was a runaway success. The tease is most common in cigarette advertising and with good reason.

Existing and widely predicted restrictions on tobacco advertising are leading the manufacturers to use advertisements which bear little or no relation to the product. Sustained advertising campaigns have persuaded much of the British public to associate three particular colours with three particular brands of cigarettes; specious verbal messages suggesting that Silk Cut are sophisticated, Benson and Hedges manly or John Player Special feminine are no longer needed.

The thinking behind the tease is that when, sooner or later, the consumer realises the point of the advert, he or she will think: 'What a clever advert and what a clever person I am to understand it!' The consumer becomes one of the club and will purchase the product as intended.

Admen used to claim that they were there to inform the public about the products that were available to them; we've come a long way from that. If, as has been estimated, we in the West are each day the target of around two thousand advertising messages, then perhaps advertisers with a new product to sell should deserve our sympathy. But do they have the right to waste our time with advertisements that, on the face of it, frequently make no sense at all? And what do their clients think of it all? Has the advertising of our consumer society finally got out of all control?

The Independent Broadcasting Authority, watchdog of Britain's commercial television, has banned the most recent advertisements for Levi 501 Jeans during children's viewing hours. They're too sexy! The commercial cost a quarter of a million pounds to make and involved the lighting expert from *Empire of the Sun*, the designer of *Cry Freedom* and a host of other talent. The latest of Levi's advertising mini-dramas featured a muscular young man who spent most of the advert not wearing his Levis and a young woman who plainly preferred him that way.

Cinema commercials are less restricted. A current advertisement, again for jeans, spices sex with violence and includes menacing punks, gnashing Dobermans and a panic-stricken girl who ends up spread-eagled against a wall. According to the man who made the advert, the sixteen to twenty year old to whom the jeans are targeted, 'does not relate exclusively to violence but aggression, both verbal and emotional, is part of his way of life'. If this is really the adolescent's taste, should advertisers be pandering to it – and in a cinema above all? The audience can choose its feature films but has no control over the advertisements it sees in the intervals.

The results of research have sent shudders down the advertising industry's collective spine. Apparently, consumers are getting bored with sex. Sexy pictures are a turn-off for men as well as women. The surprising discovery was revealed to the Market Research Society's March conference by the researchers Mullholland and Harrison. Women questioned about the models in perfume and lingerie ads said they were 'tramps' and 'unnatural'. Their boyfriends and husbands, shown glamour ads, said the models were 'too tarty'. One particular advert showed a model exposing her bra in an office; it was designed to get across the 'career girls wear our bras' message. But a typical reaction was: 'It looks like a tacky scene after an office party.'

Apparently, it's the soft, caring and realistically feminine image which most appeals to both male and female consumers. 'The women they respond to are beautiful but in an essentially ordinary way. They would not look out of place shopping in the High Street.' I wonder if that goes for the viewers who watch *Dallas* and *Dynasty* on British television.

Practitioners and apologists of advertising say that the professional merely signals the existence of artefacts and opportunities that might otherwise go undetected in the jungle of commodities. It helps us to weigh judiciously the competing merits of diverse products. It educates us into being wise and discriminating consumers. But the opposite is the case. One extraordinary by-product of the information-rich societies is the creation of a kind of unknowing, even ignorance, that is strangely at odds with the many means of communication they have at their command. It is a replica of older patterns of ignorance whereby people today have become unaware of the origin, the violence, the exploitation and pain involved in the production of their articles of daily consumption, just as the peasantry was once unaware of the forces which governed the rhythm of their lives, such as who owned the earth which they cultivated.

A new and artificial technopeasantry is in the making and it is served by advertising and its 'culture of wanting'. It legitimises all wants without hierarchies or distinctions, so that whim, caprice, desire, yearning and need become indistinguishable. Advertising is the religious art of a throwaway age. And the instant of buying is the most intense and concentrated experience that our culture is capable of offering the individual.

Comprehension

1. What is the new advertising 'tease'?
2. At what point did the WISPA bar become successful?
3. Why is the 'tease' method of advertising favoured by the tobacco industry?
4. What was the problem with the Levis advert?
5. What can be said about the taste of the cinema jeans advert?
6. What has made the advertising companies 'shudder'?
7. Why was the bra advert unsuccessful?
8. What image of woman seems to remain the favourite with the viewing public?
9. Using a dictionary where necessary, define the following

    manufacturer   client
    consumer   product
    adolescent   exploitation

10 Find a word or phrase in the text that means

member of the public
sweets or chocolate
plausible on the surface but not true
group which monitors standards of practice
to collude with or encourage something bad

Aspects of Advertising

1 Advertising, in the widest meaning of the term, takes on many distinct forms. Where, for example, is the dividing line between promotion, advertising and public relations? At one moment it informs, recommends or suggests and at the next we are encouraged, persuaded and cajoled into buying something. It serves to raise the profile of a product or company or purely to remind us of its existence so when we encounter it on a supermarket shelf we recognise it. When in doubt it is usually the familiar brand that is purchased.

Advertising is increasingly being used in the realm of political life. Not only in America are glossy and subtle high-tech videos and advertisements the order of the day. Politicians are choosing to reach millions by turning up at a television studio for an interview instead of touring the country and delivering rousing oratory. Saatchi and Saatchi became famous in Britain when they were commissioned by the Conservative Party, then in opposition, to handle and co-ordinate all party promotion in the 1979 General Election. A series of adverts was realised that filled billboards across Britain projecting the Tory message and the Election resulted in a big Conservative majority. Of course, the costs of such an advertising campaign are very high but the results can easily justify the expenditure. However, those who can most afford the high price of professional PR are probably those who need it least.

LABOUR ISN'T WORKING.

UNEMPLOYMENT OFFICE

BRITAIN'S BETTER OFF WITH THE CONSERVATIVES

* Study the words below. Sort them into pairs of near synonyms.

design	sponsoring	selling
billboard	customer	agent
artwork	endorsing	representative
poster	client	marketing

2 Credit is now being promoted and advertised as never before. People are being persuaded to buy money and then being told by other advertisements what to spend it on. Banks and Building Societies are at the forefront of this onslaught, heedless of the effect of personal debt on the social fabric and the balance of payments and a laissez-faire government refuses to take any responsibility. Artificial needs and desires are being foisted upon us and, because of the employment of evermore sophisticated techniques, we are beginning to believe that they are natural and immutable.

We now have to contend with junk mail, telephone selling and even cold visits by sales representatives to our homes in the evening. There is a new and thriving market for 'luxury' goods, often bought on credit, naturally, with the manufacturers of glassware, china, jewellery and leather-bound books promoting their products and the associated 'lifestyle' all over the place.

Designer labels have acquired special status and emanate a kind of religious aura. Any pair of jeans will not do; it has to be a pair with the correct label. Not only have we been transmogrified into habitual consumers, but we are increasingly defining ourselves and each other in terms of objects. We have become commodity fetishists. Images of consumers in adverts are largely stereotypes; they have to stand for categories of people in order to strike a bond of identification with as many of us as possible.

* Describe some of the problems caused by too much credit.

3 Public relations takes one of two forms: promotion or defence. Companies are now, in increasing numbers, demanding professional expertise to present themselves in a positive, humane and reassuring light at critical moments in their evolution. The inevitability of occasional aircraft disasters, train and road accidents put the transport industry especially at risk.

Crisis management has increased in importance because of the potentially damaging effect on companies of disasters. As the media are invariably on the spot instantly, a response must be well prepared and be delivered, preferably, by senior figures from the management. The affairs of a corporation are put under the public microscope in the ensuing search for culpability.

Many firms are now making contingency plans to meet the immediate aftermath of a disaster more effectively. They must be able to produce information that puts the company in the best possible light and makes them appear completely ingenuous. Companies are aware of the danger of leaving themselves open to accusations of covering up truths or white-washing. The days when disasters invariably spelled bad publicity, with the likely consequence of a down-turn in profitability, are over.

* Think of some recent disasters in Europe or elsewhere and describe what effect they had on the public image of the organisation concerned.

4 Advertising, on one level, is completely amoral; it is only the products that harbour values. However, to the extent that advertising encourages the proliferation of products it reinforces values. Society bestows certain values on, for example, cars, drinks and clothes. Advertisers would have us accept that the products they promote embody qualities which they are capable of imparting, such as beauty, that are alien to them. The implication is made that through ownership desirable qualities are reflected on the owner. Products are presented connected to human experience; lifestyles and sexual relationships are portrayed as being at the centre of material goods and an essential part of their meaning. In this way they are well on the way to becoming modern spiritual icons.

Consuming places you in a social group, usually a bunch of attractive, fashionable, successful, outgoing and, above all, young people. But what values do the products really embody? We are only half aware that our consumption decisions have very real repercussions on individual lives around the world. Our ever-increasing consumption of fuel in motor cars is now widely accepted to be partly responsible for the greenhouse effect.

Adverts are sometimes juxtaposed with editorial material dealing with death or starvation or some other story of human tragedy. How aware are we of the disturbing irony evident in our indiscriminate consumption of tragic factual deprivation and fantasy images of material acquisition between the covers of a product designed to entertain? Even when informing or educating, the overiding priority of most magazines and newspapers is to entertain. The factual, documentary identity of the article lends truth to adverts appearing on the same or opposite pages.

Watching television involves a similar reciprocation of values experienced and taken on board unconsciously by the viewer. Here soap operas, news and advertisements reinforce each other until all seem to occupy a twilight land of neither truth nor falsehood but a desensitising blend of both.

* Does and should an advert convey the truth about a product?

* Debate formally or informally one of the following motions

    'The advertising industry provides a lot of employment and supports a range of other industries and enterprises.'

    'Advertising is a form of art.'

    'We all have to sell ourselves to other people.'

    'Jesus was a salesman.'

    Now turn to the grammar exercises on page 81.

Listening

An advertising executive and his client are having a preliminary discussion about how best to project the new product: the CBX 550. Listen to the tape and then answer the questions.

1. What is the 'sexy' idea for selling the CBX 550?
2. How does the 'technical' approach work?
3. In the opinion of the adman, what approach appeals to the typical yuppy?
4. What is a commuter?
5. What is the final suggestion from the adman?

Language Activity

Choose a product from a magazine advertisement, and 'sell it' to members of your group. You may need a few minutes' preparation.

Media Watch

Make notes on ten advertisements from the various media that in your opinion are successful. Consider the following points

* What claims are made directly or indirectly for the product?
* What is the general 'angle' of the ad (sexy, technical, lifestyle etc)?
* Why does it appeal to you?

Compare your notes with others and discuss the differences in the advertisers' techniques.

Soft Sell   Interpretations in English

Questionnaire

Market research companies are more and more frequently employed to monitor the public's reaction to various advertisements. Below is an example of a questionnaire designed to evaluate the effectiveness of a TV commercial for an airline company.

Using a similar format, design a questionnaire to check the success of an advertising campaign you have noticed on television. Interview at least two people. Continue on a separate sheet for the longer answers.

Questions	Replies
Have you ever considered flying to Australia?	
Why / Why not?	
Can you name any airline companies which fly to Australia?	
Can you recall any advertisements in the media for airlines flying to Australia? (If yes:)	
What can you remember particularly about the advertisements?	
Do you think you might fly to Australia in the future? (If yes:)	
How will you choose the airline?	
Which TV channels do you watch the most?	
Which TV channel were you watching last night at 9.30?	
Do you think it is more important to have a comfortable or an economic flight on long journeys?	

Afterthought

Britain spends about twenty million pounds a year on libraries, museums, galleries, orchestras, the Arts Council and adult education. Three hundred and sixty five million pounds a year is spent on advertising.

Murderers or Martyrs?

unit six

Murderers or Martyrs? *Interpretations in English*

Definitions   Terrorism is... the use of violence for political ends.

British Prevention of Terrorism Act 1976

...the deliberate and systematic murder, maiming and menacing of the innocent to inspire fear for political ends.

Benjamin Yetanyahu – Israel's Ambassador to the UN

One man's terrorist is another man's freedom fighter.

It is the inalienable right of freedom-fighters to take up arms to fight their oppressors. People held in perpetual bondage could not be stopped from taking their oppressors hostage, if that became inevitable.

Tanzanian amendment to UN convention on hostages, 1977

Terrorism is... a deliberate means to an end. It is not mindless. It has objectives.

Grant Wardlaw – Australian criminologist

Terrorism is the strategy of the poor and the weak against tyrants.

Terrorism is... the threat or use of violence designed to create extreme anxiety in a target group larger than the immediate victims with the purpose of coercing that group into acceding to the political demands of the perpetrators.

Grant Wardlaw

Read the text and as you do so consider the following questions. Remember, you don't have to understand every word in order to answer them.

1 What characterises the modern terrorist?
2 How powerful a force is terrorism in the contemporary world?

The Power of Terror

One might be forgiven for deducing from newspaper and TV reports that terrorism is a new phenomenon. But the experts, however they may disagree on their definitions, are unanimous in their insistence that terrorism has been with us for well over one hundred years. Soon after the middle of the last century there were well organised terrorist groups fighting the Tsarist government in Russia and British rule in India. Not long after, anarchists were launching attacks in Italy and France and Irish nationalists were trying, with some success, to bomb the British into granting home rule in Ireland.

However terrorism is to be defined, modern terrorists are much better at it than their predecessors for two main reasons: first, with more effective and rapid news reporting the terrorist is assured 'the oxygen of publicity', as the British Prime Minister once put it. Hand-held 'minicams', satellite technology and the 'faxing' of conferences and interviews feed the world media's need for exciting news material and thereby make, overnight, an international star of the most obscure activist; and the myth-making tendencies of the modern media make living legends out of the likes of the mercenary Carlos the Jackal and Abu Nidal the extremist Palestinian leader.

If the claim is justified that terrorism is often the only means of publicising injustice, then the journalist is the terrorist's partner in crime. Journalists may claim that they are doing no more than holding up a mirror to events, but it is at least arguable that, without publicity, terrorism would lose its raison d'être. Of course, then we enter the realm of freedom of speech and it is interesting to recall the wave of controversy that broke over Thatcher's banning of the reporting of direct speech of IRA members and suspected terrorists. Could the cost of defeating terrorism be the loss of our hard-won civil liberties? Or is there a real danger that in trying to respond adequately to the threat we lose our moral high ground and sink to the same level of degradation as the people we are trying to defeat?

The modern terrorist's second ace is the huge destructive power of modern weaponry. The Scorpion machine pistol which is capable of firing over five hundred rounds per minute, the best selling Kalashnikov AK–47 rifle and the plastic and aluminium Armalite AR–15 are relatively cheap and easily available; and they can all guarantee death on a massive scale. Even more frightening are the surface to air SAM–57 missiles, rocket propelled grenades and Semtex high explosive which have been found in the possession of terrorist groups. The high cost of such sophisticated weapons is not prohibitive: one of the world's best known terrorist groups has an estimated income of around nine hundred million dollars a year.

It is only a matter of time before a terrorist group manages to acquire its own nuclear 'deterrent'. The Lockerbie air disaster in fact was reported to have occurred in terrifying proximity to a nuclear power plant. A catastrophe potentially worse than Chernobyl was reportedly avoided by minutes. Despite the universal acceptance of the 1989 UN Paris Convention's ban on chemical weapons, already there is talk of chemical weapons being supplied to rebel forces in Somalia.

A well-funded organisation could plausibly even construct their own nuclear device perhaps using the instructions published (with all the necessary diagrams) by a twenty-year old American student some years ago. It remains to be seen whether these disturbing possibilities and the increasing list of lives lost through violent terrorist attack will encourage governments to try to deal seriously with the underlying causes of terrorism as well as declaring their determined intention to punish the perpetrators.

Glossary

	living legends	people whose deeds are highly publicised and often exaggerated
	Semtex	an odourless, virtually undetectable plastic explosive
	ace	a winning card, ie advantage
	stockpile	a large store of armaments

Comprehension

1. Give two examples of terrorist activity in the nineteenth century.
2. What were the Irish nationalists trying to achieve through violent means?
3. Explain the meaning of the phrase the *oxygen of publicity*.
4. Give examples of modern technology that help the cause of the terrorist.
5. In what sense can journalists be said to be the partners in crime?
6. Why do you think some terrorist organisations are able to afford expensive weapons?
7. How might the civil liberties of the general public be affected in the war against terrorism?
8. What are the main differences between nineteenth century terrorist groups and those of modern times?
9. What do you think is meant by the *underlying cause of terrorism*?

Murderers or Martyrs? *Interpretations in English*

10 In pairs or groups work on your own definition of terrorism. You may use the following ideas to shape your discussion

   a) Are terrorists usually from one political wing in terms of European politics?

   b) Does such a thing as 'state terrorism' and 'official terrorism' exist?

   c) Can terrorism ever be justified?

   d) What is the difference between terrorism and warfare?

Consider cases from your own country if appropriate.

Profiles

Read the descriptions below of three well-known terrorist groups. Make brief notes on them including the following information

* when the group was founded
* its main aims
* its supporters and leaders

1 The Palestinian Liberation Organisation was founded in 1964 with the aim of providing an Palestinian Arab homeland and removing the state of Israel which, until recently, it regarded as illegal. The PLO is actually made up of a number of Palestinian groups, some moderate others extreme. Despite many challenges Yassah Arafat remains chairman and leader. The PLO enjoys overwhelming support from the Palestinian people and since 1974 has been recognised by Arab nations as 'the sole legitimate representative of the Palestinian people'.

In that same year Arafat addressed the UN General Assembly in New York where he proffered an olive branch in one hand and a gun in the other. The following year the UN accepted a resolution denouncing Zionism as 'racism' and gave the PLO 'observer status' on UN committees. Some PLO factions rejected Arafat's diplomacy and continue the military struggle against Israel. The Palestinians residing in Israel can vote but their political activity is strictly limited. The one and a half million in the occupied West Bank and Gaza have no political rights. Israel continues to refuse face to face negotiations with the PLO on the grounds that they are a 'terrorist organisation'.

2 The African National Congress started in 1912 as the South African Native National Congress to protect the black populace against the injustices of the white regime. Its chosen method was organised passive resistance propounded by Mahatma Ghandi, then a young lawyer practising in South Africa. One of the ANC's early leaders was Chief Albert Luthuli, who was awarded the Nobel Peace Prize in 1960. A year after this award the ANC was banned by the South African government. Under its new leaders, lawyers Nelson Mandela and Oliver Tambo, the ANC spawned a military wing called Umkonto Ve Sizwe ('spear of the nation') to carry out acts of sabotage.

More recently the organisation has resorted to assassination and terrorism, in response to which South African security forces have regularly struck at ANC bases in Zambia. The goal of the ANC is the destruction of the system of 'racial capitalism' in South Africa under which the vast majority of the country's people have no political rights.

Interpretations in English Murderers or Martyrs?

3 The Irish Republican Army came about during the 'troubles' which broke out in Dublin in 1916 and led ultimately to the establishment of an independent Ireland in 1921. The six counties of Northern Ireland, where Protestant descendants of Scots immigrants still form a majority, remained British. In the 30s and 50s, the IRA waged terrorist campaigns in support of their demands for a united Ireland. Although the government of Eire (independent Ireland) also supports the cause of Irish unity, the IRA has been banned in the south because of the violent means it espouses.

The IRA became active again in the 1960s in support of the Northern Ireland Civil Rights Association. The Catholic minority in the north commonly suffered victimisation and discrimination at the hands of the Royal Ulster Constabulary. Protestant hardliners tried to establish pogroms against the Catholics and when the IRA joined in to protect Catholic communities, open warfare ensued. Many new recruits from Catholic or 'Republican' communities swelled the ranks of the movement, but disagreements over policy led, in 1970, to a split between the Marxist Official IRA, the militaristic Provisional IRA and the small but violent Irish National Liberation Army. Despite disagreement over methods, the shared objectives remain the expulsion of the 'Brits' in Northern Ireland and the establishment of a united Ireland in the face of violent opposition from the Protestant majority in the North that has, in turn, produced its own violent groupings.

The IRA – especially the 'Provos' – are well supported by Irish Americans and are well armed with weapons allegedly supplied by Libya. Violent indiscriminate attacks continue to claim victims among the British security forces and members of the public in Ireland, Britain and, indeed, throughout Europe.

Now turn to the grammar exercises on page 82.

Listening

In May 1984 American Presbyterian Missionary Benjamin Weir, a veteran of 31 years in the Lebanon was taken hostage. He spent sixteen months in captivity and on his release started to write a book about the experience. The book is called *Hostage Bound, Hostage Free*. In it he includes some of the conversations he had with his captors, members of the Islamic Jihad (*Islamic Holy War*) group. By the end of his captivity, Benjamin Weir's questioners were bringing the book *English for Beginners* into the interrogations with them and treating the sessions as English lessons.

The recorded conversation took place during the early days of his captivity. Two of his captors have come to question him. The second captor asks for the prisoner's name. Listen to the tape and answer the questions below.

1. How was Benjamin Weir employed in the Lebanon?
2. What information did his captors seek from him?
3. Describe the attitude of the members of Islamic Jihad and their methods of interrogation.
4. How did the prisoner respond to the questioning? Consider whether he was

sincere	clever
courageous	truthful
naive	intelligent
reckless	resigned

5. Explain the meaning of the following words

pastor	theology
quandary	salve

unit six 45

Murderers or Martyrs? *Interpretations in English*

Media Watch

Collect examples from newspapers and magazines of stories dealing with terrorism. Make a note of the broad aims of the group as far as they are apparent and other information given. Compare the profile with groups described in the previous section.

Language Activity

Choose one of the following motions as a subject for debate

'This house supports the re-introduction of capital punishment for terrorist crimes.'

'This house believes in the right of the weak and exploited to use violent means in the struggle against oppression.'

'This house believes that world peace is threatened above all by state-sponsored terrorism.'

'This house believes that terrorism should be stamped out at all costs.'

Questionnaire

Ask six people the meaning of the term *terrorist* and request an example. Compare your definitions and examples with those of other members of the class.

Afterthought

'How do you statistically reduce your chance of being on a plane containing a terrorist bomb?'

'Bring your own bomb: the chance of there being two on one plane is extremely remote.'

Defence of the Realm

unit seven

Read the text and as you do so consider the following questions. Remember, you don't have to understand every word in order to answer them.

1. How have relations recently changed between East and West?
2. What is the INF treaty?

The Foreign Secretary Speaks

Nato – the North Atlantic Treaty Organisation – is the cornerstone of the defence of the West. In this article, a former Secretary General reflects on the state of the Alliance and the challenges it faces.

Back in 1984, East and West were hardly on speaking terms. Public opinion had become disillusioned at what was seen as an endless arms race. Support for Utopian and escapist alternatives offered by unilateral disarmers grew, although solidarity in implementing Nato's 1979 decision on the intermediate-range nuclear foces was maintained.

Few could have predicted the strides which would soon be made in East-West relations and in arms control. Hardly anyone could have predicted that Soviet troops would leave Afghanistan; that President Reagan and Mr Gorbachev would have held four summit meetings; that all this US/Soviet activity would have been carried over into the work of Nato; that the first arms control agreement in history to remove a whole category of nuclear weapons would be signed and ratified, with the prospect of further progress across a range of disarmament issues greater than ever before.

While the West has taken the lead, we cannot take all the credit for these developments, but I do believe that without Nato solidarity and the consistent application of a sound policy, based on the complementary principles of security and dialogue with the East we should not now be in such a good position to exploit the opportunities and, indeed, to meet the challenges posed by the present Kremlin leadership.

The focus of general public opinion is of course on whether and how this climate can be used to make the world a safer place through arms reductions and lower defence budgets. There is a danger of euphoria clouding common sense. After all, only 4% of the nuclear weapons in the world will be removed by the INF treaty.

The Soviet Union and its allies continue to enjoy military superiority, particularly at the conventional level. Further arms agreements will therefore need to include asymmetric reductions, as did the INF agreement. Agreements will also need to embody intrusive and effective verification arrangements which are easy for the West with its more open society, but much more difficult for the Soviet Union. Above all we shall need to negotiate from adequate strength, in nuclear as well as conventional forces.

What alliance governments are finding hard to avoid is involuntary or 'structural disarmament'. I mean by that the erosion of our deterrent because of unwillingness to provide the resources necessary to maintain adequate defence. In this sense we are victims of our own success because the progress in East-West relations and its impact on public opinion, have made support for defence spending harder to win.

The Soviet nuclear modernisation programme continues apace. Expenditure on procurement continues to grow at 3% a year, despite Gorbachev's peace rhetoric. In these circumstances, the West cannot take the risk of running down its own forces or of expecting to achieve arms control agreements which preserve our security if we enter into the negotiations from positions of weakness with nothing to bargain in return.

Progress in East-West relations has in fact been a story of successive Western initiatives that the Soviet Union has eventually come round to accepting. Yet it is all too easy for Nato to be portrayed as the one on the defensive. Sixteen democracies inevitably move more slowly that a centralised power like the Soviet Union and when they do move it is with an inner strength which communism can only envy. But there is perhaps room for speeding up our responses and it is in this area of public perceptions and public policy that I suspect the greatest challenge will lie in the future.

Comprehension

1. Explain the expression *to be on speaking terms*.
2. What does the writer think of supporters of unilateral disarmament?
3. Is the West responsible for the positive developments in East-West relations? Explain.
4. *There is a danger of euphoria clouding common sense.* Rewrite this sentence using your own words.
5. What do you understand by *intrusive verification*?
6. What conditions are necessary for negotiations to continue?
7. What is *procurement*?
8. Find an antonymic (opposite) expression for *to run down its forces*.
9. Why is it easy to portray Nato as being on the defensive?
10. Why should Western democracies be the envy of the communist regimes?

Big Business

1 One inevitable aspect of defence is the arms business and the conflicting interests of industry and government. Any lasting peace in the Middle East would bring to a close one of the most lucrative chapters of the arms business. Iran and Iraq, for example, purchased arms worth more than £10 billion a year to sustain the war effort – around one quarter of all arms exports. Peace would also mean lean times for France and China, who have both made millions out of Middle East conflicts, and for the illegal arms dealers who will see the end of the bonanza.

The Iran/Iraq war came when the export market for arms was declining and provided a useful outlet for companies and countries desperate to keep flagging industries working. Although most countries in the West and East remained officially neutral in the war, an underground network of dummy companies, shady dealers and willing shippers sprang up, often with the tacit approval of governments.

The scramble for contracts and the opportunity to make large profits led to a rash of illegal sales, with many companies selling to both sides. According to the Stockholm International Peace Research Institute, 53 countries have supplied arms to Iran and Iraq with 28 selling to both sides.

The war graphically illustrated the amoral nature of the arms business. Israel, an enemy of both Iran and Iraq, sold weapons captured from the Palestine Liberation Organisation in Lebanon to Iran. South Africa supplied the G5 artillery system and ammunition to both sides in exchange for oil. Some countries such as China and North Korea have developed a big arms export industry as a result of the war. Many Western countries, which remain officially neutral, continued secretly to sell arms. Sweden, Italy and Austria have been involved in illegal sales.

The prospect of the war spilling over into neighbouring countries, such as Kuwait and Saudi Arabia, also led to increased arms purchases, including a Saudi order for more than £15 billion worth of British fighters, minesweepers and helicopters.

Countries such as France and the United States sold arms in part to secure the release of hostages held by Iranian-sponsored terrorists and in part to gain influence for economic and strategic purposes. Ironically, those countries that compromised over arms sales are the ones most likely to benefit from the billions of pounds of business now up for grabs as both sides begin the process of rebuilding their shattered economies. Britain maintained a hard line on arms sales and is consequently likely to be near the end in the long queue for contracts.

* The period from 1945 to the present day is often said to be the longest uninterrupted era of peace since the sixteenth century. Find a map of the world and mark any areas of international conflict that you and the rest of the class are aware of.

Consider these two statements

'Britain spends 5% of GNP on defence and the defence industry is responsible for some three million jobs.'

'The cost of one F–16 fighter is equivalent to the price of a hospital.'

1. Do you think these figures are accurate?
2. How important is defence
    a) for the economy?
    b) for security?
3. Debate the motion 'This house believes that defence spending is the price to be paid for peace.'

Battle Scenario

2 Even the most convinced pacifists may change their minds if their own country was attacked. But would they be able to do anything? Let's look at a possible scenario for an upcoming conflict.

'Tension had been mounting in Europe for some weeks. Both Warsaw Pact and Nato forces had been placed on the alert and although there had been no attacks, the allies were taking no chances. The evening before, reports had filtered through to Nato HQ of attacks on bases and senior political and military figures.

These had been the opening shots fired by Soviet Spetsnaz commandos attacking radar stations, airfields and missile sites in Britain and the rest of Europe. Most of them had entered the country secretly by plane, ship and concealed as freight aboard long-distance lorries. It took only a few raids to create confusion.

At 6.30 am on Monday April 18, allied airborne early warning aircraft (AWACS) picked up the first clear signs that World War Three was about to start. In rapid succession the radar spotted the departure of enemy aircraft from the Smolensk airbase. Fighters and bombers flew in two separate flight formations, one heading north-east around Norway, the other going directly over the Baltic Sea. Both formations were clearly directed at the British Isles.

The massive AWACS computers processed the data to produce details of the numbers, types and courses of the enemy aircraft. The details were instantly sent by automatic data link to RAF Strike Command at High Wycombe, 25 miles north of London and to the other key radar ground stations on the mainland.

The nerve centre that controls Britain's air defences in war today has hardly changed since it was built in 1938. That morning, the large screen on the far wall presented a depressing picture. Three waves of enemy aircraft, each more than 150 strong, were heading for Britain from different directions. The radar being used to monitor them was, in some areas, more than 33 years old and was often unable to cope with the mass of information.

The first exchanges in the war were critical. Within minutes of the first aircraft being detected, all the air raid warning alarm buttons had been pressed to warn the nation of imminent attack. Less than thirty minutes from the first aircraft being detected on the radar screens, Britain was at war.'

The result of this wargame showed that, after two days, ten of Britain's twelve major airfields had been hit, although eight were back in action within twelve hours. Fifteen British Tornado fighters and eight Phantoms had been shot down and several others badly damaged. However, the Soviets suffered even heavier losses, running four to one in favour of the British. The Soviets could have virtually destroyed the RAF within four more days of similar attack but their losses would have been unacceptably high. The RAF had achieved its objective which was not to win but to buy time to force the enemy to think again and to adopt new and untested tactics that would lead them to make even greater mistakes.

a) Is this scenario over-optimistic?

b) Do you think that the result of these heavy losses would be the use of nuclear weapons by the Warsaw Pact?

c) Explain the implications of the idea of *unacceptably high losses*.

d) Is it dangerous to assume automatically that the Soviet Union is the enemy? What affect does this have on public opinion?

e) Is to talk about the unspeakable the height of irresponsibility because it encourages the idea that another world war would somehow be 'winnable'? Does providing a rehearsal make the reality more conceivable in the public mind, therefore less implausible and more likely to happen?

A Civil Connection?

3 A common argument to justify high spending on defence is that benefits 'trickle down' into the civil sector. One professor of International Studies pointed out, however, that the country with the strongest economy in the world (apart from the US), namely Japan, has no defence industry to speak of. Do you think that the trickle-down argument is valid?

Look at the following five developments in defence technology and try to find civil spin-offs.

high energy lasers
sonar
transatmospheric aircraft
electromagnetic rail gun
over-the-horizon radar

unit seven

Defence of the Realm *Interpretations in English*

Biowars

4 A 1982 US Army study concluded: 'One other aspect of the future battle is drawn from the growing proliferation of nuclear, chemical and biological weapons coupled with the enemy's apparent permissive attitude regarding employment of these weapons. It is imperative that forces plan from the outset to fight on this 'conventional-nuclear-chemical-biological-electronic battlefield.'

* What circumstances, if any, can justify the use of chemical and biological weapons?

1. Try and find out as a group which countries, eg in Europe, have compulsory military service and contrast them with other countries where the armed forces are voluntary. What do you think are the benefits and drawbacks of the two systems?

2. Split into small groups and draw a rough map of Europe. Take one country in Europe and decide how you would attack it if you were a military planner. Which countries would you sacrifice to defend it? Where would you base your deterrent forces? Apply your reasoning to another country. What, if anything, is different?

3. In current scenarios, the future enemy of the West is the Warsaw Pact; is this still true? Can you think of any other potential enemies? How reliable an ally is the USA? Should countries like Britain and France retain an independent nuclear deterrent? Assess the threat to Western interests of fundamental Islamic fervour.

4. Unilateral disarmament is an issue that continues to divide public opinion (generally on the left). Divide up into two groups, one at each end of the room: those for and those against such a strategy. Which is the larger group?

5. Look at the advert on the next page. How does it go about attracting recruits? Explain why you think it succeeds or otherwise in its aim to make the work seem appealing. Compare the style with that of similar literature in your own or another country.

6. What impact has the Falklands campaign had on the two countries involved?

Now turn to the grammar exercises on page 83.

Listening

Listen to the tape recording of Prime Minister's Question Time in the House of Commons and try to describe briefly the circumstances that have given rise to the controversy

Media Watch

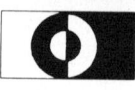

A Choose two papers of different shades of opinion (eg *The Daily Telegraph* and *The Guardian* or two other newspapers you know) and compare their coverage of defence.

* How much space is given to defence issues?

* Do opinions on spending differ?

* Can you detect the papers' attitudes to the military?

* Overall, do you have the impression that the press either in Britain or your own country is proud of the armed forces or that it considers them to be a necessary evil?

Interpretations in English **Defence of the Realm**

B Look at the army publicity below and explain in what ways you think it would succeed in attracting new recruits and why it might be less successful. Compare the approach evident here with similar examples of advertisements for military personnel in one or more other countries.

MEET THE PROFESSIONALS

In today's Army we need men who can master the high-powered technology of modern weapons and equipment. But these same men must be able to keep going on active service for days on end when everything's against them — as British soldiers have always done. It's because we're trained for both these things that we are known as the Professionals.

Would you measure up?

Make no mistake, there's no better life for the right man. We can teach you a trade or skill and pay you well even while you're learning. We can offer you a career where promotion comes as soon as you're up to it, and the way's clear right to the top. We can give you confidence, self-reliance, the ability to look the world in the eye. We can offer you travel, adventure, sport, good pay — and good friends.

But the rewards don't come easily. Things that are worth having seldom do.

In this book we tell you about the modern Army, the jobs it has to do, the trades you can learn and how we teach you, your career prospects, your day-to-day life, the demands we make and the fun that's on offer.

Read it and think about it carefully. Then, if you're interested, have a talk with one of the Professionals at your nearest Army Careers Information Office. You'll find the address in the telephone book under 'Army'.

unit seven

Language Activity

A Acquire a set of Snakes and Ladders and study the rules carefully. Then devise your own 'military' version.

Prepare a list of negative situations which relate to the snake squares (eg 'Your defence budget is cut') and a list of positive situations for the ladder squares (eg 'You successfuly develop a new weapon'). Design and make your board game with a partner and then exchange games with another pair.

B Split up into small groups and choose one of the following questions for discussion. Appoint a secretary to make notes on your discussion and report back to the class. The secretary should try and get an opinion from every member of the group.

* Why do you think war tends to be waged by men not women?
* What, if any, is the difference between patriotism and nationalism?
* Is war a consequence of nationalist sentiments?
* How significant are the names given to instruments of war?
* In the past going to war was considered a noble activity. Has the situation changed and, if so, why?
* Do you feel that the availability of toy weapons directed specifically at boys plays a role in reinforcing sexual stereotyping that is detrimental to social relations and, ultimately, could push the world towards Armageddon?
* Explain the phrases below and give reasons for agreeing/disagreeing with them.

    Better dead than red
    Better red than dead
    Protect and survive
    Protest and survive

* Do you think it is either possible or wise to construct imagined war-time scenarios?

Afterthought

The arms race is based on an optimistic view of technology and a pessimistic view of man. It assumes that there is no limit to the ingenuity of science and no limit to the devilry of human beings.

I.F. Stone

* Is war inevitable?

This is `I.T.`!

Read the text and as you do so consider the following questions. Remember, you don't have to understand every word in order to answer them.

1. How powerful are computers today?
2. How does computer intelligence differ from human intelligence?

The Intelligent Machine

Among the most oddly-named technocrats of the computer age are the 'knowledge processors', aka 'information engineers'. But they manage one of the most obviously useful applications of modern computer technology: the Expert System – software which contains the sum of human expertise in one particular subject area, such as medical diagnosis, car maintenance or chemical analysis. If, on some future visit to your bank or health centre, you find yourself talking to a computer instead of the normal human being, you will have the information engineers to thank.

Ford of America are installing an Expert System to help Ford mechanics throughout the USA pinpoint engine faults. Until now they have had to phone Ford's engine specialist Gordy Kujawski in Michigan with their knottiest problems. From now on they will simply plug into a nationwide computer system which duplicates exactly the reasoning Kujawski would use to solve the problem. US Intelligence have an Expert System which contains the specialist knowledge of several international anti-terror experts; it is said to have predicted terrorist attacks on several targets in Western Europe. Perhaps the most advanced Expert System is that of the American photocopy company Xerox. RIC (for Remote Interactive Communications), when installed in a copier, routinely monitors the machine's performance, diagnosing abnormalities and predicting failure. The machine's operators may then be told that, unless they make this or that adjustment, their machine will fail a week tomorrow.

There are currently about 2,000 Expert Systems in daily use, and the number is increasing by 50% per year. In tests, an early medical diagnostic Expert System proved 65% accurate, in contrast to an average of just 52% for a panel of human specialists. Its bedside manner left something to be desired, however.

The late British mathematician Alan Turing once said that a machine was intelligent if it was clever enough to be mistaken for a human being. Ask a sausage-making machine what a sausage is; if it can give an answer, and one that we might expect from a human sausage-maker, then we must conclude that the machine can think. According to the current director of the Turing Institute, their founder's definition has stood the test of time. However, Dr Mowforth has his own definition of machine intelligence: 'If you can demonstrate that a machine can learn, then it is intelligent.' This is very similar to the standard AI technique of heuristic search used, for example, to deduce fundamental laws of nature from raw scientific data or to synthesise rules of behaviour from given examples.

Because of their speed, modern computers can use the heuristic search technique effectively to make genuine discoveries in medicine, chemical analysis and many other fields. But is this really 'thinking'? According to some experts it is. The philosopher Kenneth Craik, for example, suggested that the brain 'thinks' in much the same way that today's computers work – by manipulating symbols (words, pictures or whatever) of what is being thought about. A strong challenge to this 'brain-as-computer' approach comes from an unexpected quarter: California's 'silicon valley', where Terry Winograd and Fernando Flores are based.

For them human thought is part of a complex interaction with the environment from which 'thought' cannot be artificially separated. The brain's understanding of 'spoon', for example, does not involve pictures or words in the mind, but a complex configuration of brain cells which has, at some time in the past (when first learning the word or seeing the object, perhaps), corresponded to 'spoon'.

Even more confusion surrounds the concept of 'artificial intelligence'. A computer expert who recently reviewed six new books on machine intelligence concluded that there is no coherent discipline of artificial intelligence – as there is for mathematics or logic, for example. He found that the definition of AI differed from one book to the next. AI, for example, could be used to: write learning programs for knowledge acquisition and retrieval (so-called 'expert systems'), teach cognitive skills to a computer, produce intelligence tests, and so on and so on.

It has been cynically suggested that such a well-funded but confusingly diversified subject area as AI has come about because, about 15 years ago, the US military establishment decided that AI was where the future lay; the Pentagon hinted that scientists engaged on AI projects could expect generous financial assistance and, not unnaturally, many scientists working on many diverse projects all claimed to be engaged on AI research.

Glossary

aka	also known as
heuristic	by trial and error
routinely	regularly
'silicon valley'	area in California famous for its computer industry
AI	Artificial Intelligence

Comprehension

1. What is a 'technocrat'?
2. Explain the aim of installing an Expert System.
3. How do Xerox use their Expert System?
4. How successful was the medical diagnostic Expert System?
5. Explain the phrase *its bedside manner left something to be desired*.
6. Give a definition of machine intelligence.
7. What do you understand by *heuristic search technique*?
8. Comment on Winograd and Flores' views on human versus computer 'thought'.
9. What is the problem with the discipline of Artificial Intelligence?
10. Why, according to some people, is the field of AI now so diverse?

This is I.T.!
Interpretations in English

Chips with all the trimmings

1   During the Falklands War, ships of the British Task Force sustained heavy damage from Exocet missiles, in spite of being packed with the latest in computing technology; crewmen watched aghast as the slow-moving missiles approached them while their defences did nothing to stop them. The reason for this computer failure is now known: the computers' 'reasoning' went as follows:

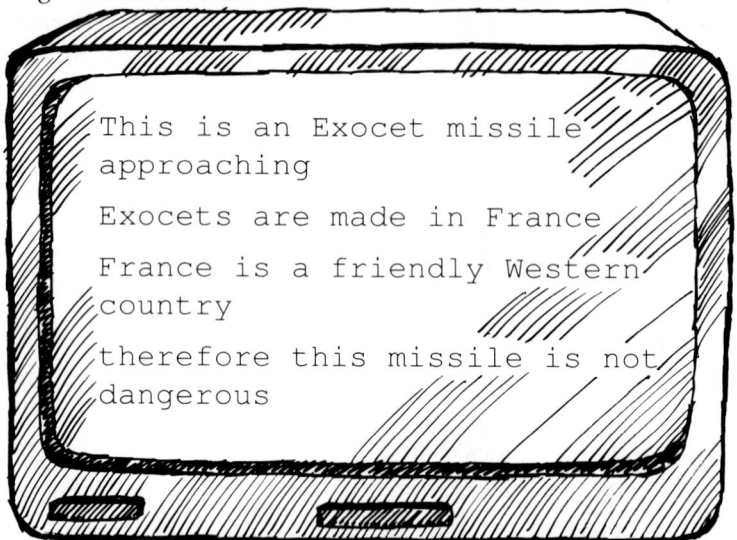

```
This is an Exocet missile
approaching
Exocets are made in France
France is a friendly Western
country
therefore this missile is not
dangerous
```

Modern computers are notoriously single-minded: they will do exactly what they are asked to do, but no more. They can process one piece of information at a time and in a limited number of ways. Which is why the race is now on to develop the so-called fifth generation computer, the neural computer.

This is a computer whose silicon chips are designed to behave like the nerve cells of the human brain, allowing the passage of data through many different connections simultaneously. Such a computer will be able to mimic the decision-making powers of the human brain. It will not necessarily be better than traditional computers at tasks like calculating (where it may be inclined to guess the answer rather than work it out exactly), it will be better at tasks where context is important or there are no definite rules. It will also be able learn from its own mistakes.

An unforeseen corollary to this machine intelligence is machine personality. A neural computer built at Imperial College, London, has startled its creators by going on strike. It refuses to co-operate when asked to do a job it considers too easy. 'You might say it had an attack of boredom,' says one member of the team.

This, and other events suggest that the next generation of computers will have to be taught good behaviour before being given any real jobs to do. 'Neural computers are a little unruly sometimes. We don't know enough about them to put them in charge of, say, a nuclear reactor,' said another team-member.

A Surfeit of Information

2   A bogus computer programme which, it appears, was deliberately created by a student, has crippled hundreds of computers working on defence projects in the United States. The computer 'virus' as it's called, also forced the shutdown of computers at the space agency NASA and a nuclear weapons laboratory. This rogue programme caused the latest major breach of computer security by a new generation of hackers.

Several new computer viruses have arrived in Britain in the last year, including the Italian virus suspected to be originally from the University of Turin (an anti-virus programme was obtained from the same university) and the Swiss Hacking Association virus. In a Glasgow hospital last year the computer in the intensive care unit was disrupted by viruses and the terminal rooms at Brighton Polytechnic have now been infected for a year.

In order to counter the problem there are three options. You can develop anti-virus vaccines, redesign your computer or outlaw the hacker. Hacking and writing viruses is still legal in Europe and the writers of viruses even hold conventions and produce information packs. Such organisations have names such as Nightmare Software and Chaos.

A virus enters the system without warning on a disk or through a network line. It's programmed to attach itself to codes inside and hijacks the computer's own copying mechanism to reproduce itself. Infected software is passed on and the invisible virus spreads.

Infected

3

'When I first realised I was infected by a virus I was shocked. I thought it would never happen to me!'

A biological virus provides a particularly good, logical analogy for a computer virus as a computer is a logical analogy of a brain.

One of the characteristics of the AIDS virus is that it actually inserts itself into human beings and disappears from sight. It's extremely difficult to detect because it looks so much like the genetic code of its host cell. Some computer viruses resemble the AIDS virus in that they're terribly slow to manifest themselves. Their delayed action may tick away like a time bomb and they replicate quietly without causing any apparent damage, perhaps for years.

The new invaders by-pass vaccines by being programmed to alter their code form, or to enter through different routes. The new wave of infection can spread through bootleg copies of popular computer games. The Trojan Horse invader, a particular form of virus, has already caused damage in important institutions such as the large firm of accountants, Price-Waterhouse. Can banks, for example, admit computer error or the presence of a virus in their systems without sacrificing the confidence of the customer?

The virus problem is definitely going to get worse. The existing viruses will spread – which is what they're designed to do. Up till now we've been very lucky, the kind of viruses we've seen have been fairly innocuous, the worst they have done is to cause a few programmes to crash. But potentially viruses could be programmed to be far more malevolent. One could even imagine a scenario where intelligence organisations and corporations deliberately engineered viruses to attack one another – and that's a fairly horrific prospect. We can only hope that the antidote business will be able to meet the challenge.

The Moon Landing

4

The dramatic success of the first moon landing was a hair's breadth from catastrophe. During the historical attempt to land the spacecraft on the moon's surface, the automatic landing procedure failed. Fortunately NASA had installed a facility which enabled the astronauts to switch off the computer and carry out the landing manually. This alternative of steering by hand narrowly averted a terrible fate – the space travellers locked in a perpetual orbit of the moon.

This is I.T.! *Interpretations in English*

An analysis of the problem found that the breakdown was a consequence of a mistake in a line of coding in the computer program that controlled the touchdown. The writer had omitted a comma.

* Write about computers in relation to one of the following
  a) unemployment
  b) freedom
  c) alienation
  d) elitism

* If computers are made by people can they ever be free from human error?

* Explain the impact of computers on freedom of information and other civil liberties.

Now turn to the grammar exercises on page 84.

Listening

Perhaps one of the most brilliant portrayals of a computer was created by Stanley Kubrick in his film of the mid nineteen sixties entitled *2001: A Space Odyssey* which was based on the novel by Arthur C. Clarke. The mystery of man, man-made intelligence and a transcendent intelligence is explored but, unsurprisingly, not explained. The problematic relationship between man and machine is highlighted in another episode of Dr Frankenstein and the Monster.

The computer is called Hal and malfunctions at a critical point during the mission to Jupiter. The voyage was begun in an attempt to find the secret of a strange object – obviously created by intelligent life – discovered beneath the surface of the moon. This monolithic artifact emitted a strong signal directly towards the planet Jupiter. The most advanced computer to have been constructed, which had never been known to make a mistake, was in charge of the mission.

However, this summit of man's achievement fails at the critical moment but events are taken over by a higher unseen intelligence and the protagonists reach their goal in spite of the failure of mere human technology. In a moving scene, the hero switches off the computer in a bid to save the mission and the layers of Hal's intelligence are unpeeled and discarded like an onion as, one by one, the modules of its 'brain' are removed. The death of the computer has the same emotional charge as if the film was dealing with the demise of a sympathetic human character. The computer begs him to stop and, reduced to the capacity of an infant, sings a nursery rhyme that evidently played a part in the programming/training of the machine. Hal says at one point: 'I can feel my mind going... '.

The recorded dialogue takes place after the crew first suspect that all is not well with the computer that they and the mission are relying on.

Listen to the recording and answer the following questions

1 Why does mission control suspect a computer error?
2 Why does Hal blame human error?

Language Activity

HAL stands for Heuristic Algorithmic Logic and the name of a large computer manufacturer is spelled by taking the three letters of the English alphabet that follow the letters H, A, L.

A Try and 'crack' the following acronyms which are coded in a similar way

EAH	OCSENU	CCD
PAC	GGE	PUBO

B Take the following acronyms and, in groups, suggest some names of organisations that would fit. Have a vote on the best ideas.

VAL	CLIC	CIMO
TUSK	NAPPI	CRASH

Domesday

In 1066 William the Conqueror invaded Britain. Nineteen years later 'King' William ordered the compilation of a complete survey of England in order to ascertain the extent of the lands he now owned. The result was a record of life in 11th century England which contained the names of villages, towns, farms and the people who lived and worked there. It detailed the value of the land, the number of sheep and cattle that grazed on it – and even mentioned the physical aspects of the countryside, such as fishponds and lakes. All this information went into the 2nd volume of the Domesday Book. Much survived and is on permanent display at the Public Records Office in Kingsway, London.

Now, 900 years after William's survey, a modern investigation is under way: the Domesday Project. It is the result of two years' work by professional researchers and approximately 15,000 schools and community groups: over one million people put in 22,000 person years to create the record; it is estimated that it would take one person over seven years to read all the information which has been collected.

The original Domesday Book was written on parchment with quill pen. The new Domesday Project is contained on a series of compact discs which include photographs, clips of video and sound, as well as text. Information can be summoned to the screen in a matter of seconds.

The Domesday Video Disk System will be of value to students and researchers, historians and, indeed, to anyone else with an interest in English society in the late 20th century. In 900 years, perhaps our descendants will be as grateful to us as we are for William's original record of life in England.

* Imagine that you are responsible for collecting ten items that, on discovery in one hundred years' time, would best convey the nature of European life in the late twentieth century. Which objects would you choose and why?

Media Watch

Find as many examples as you can of advertisements for jobs in the field of computers. Make a list of typical job titles and try and find out some simple job definitions.

This is I.T.! Interpretations in English

Questionnaire

Carry out the following questionnaire and analyse the results to discover the pattern of computer knowledge across gender and generations.

Question	Response
Do you know anything about computers?	
What is a computer?	
Do you consider yourself to be computer-literate?	
Do you know the difference between hardware and software?	
Can you operate a computer?	
Can you program a computer?	

Afterthought

HACKERS

I don't think I'm EVER going to lick this TERROR of computers...

A single careless keystroke can ruin YEARS of work, &...

Excuse me Professor, but there's a phone call for you.

unit eight

Training for Life?

Read the text and as you do so consider the following questions. Remember, you don't have to understand every word in order to answer them.

1 How does Britain appear to differ from other countries in its approach to education and training?
2 What particular skills are lacking among the British workforce?

Making the Grade

Britain has never been able – or willing – to provide effective training for its workforce, which is one reason why today's skills shortage is so acute. The situation will dull the country's competitive edge and, unless remedied, will eventually relegate Britain to the status of a second – or third – rank economic power.

As far back as 1884, the Samuelson commission concluded that other industrial countries were adapting better to industrial and structural change than Britain. One hundred years on, the problem remains unsolved. This is mainly because the link-up between vocational training and education policy is not given sufficient emphasis or priority. The National Curriculum Council has warned of the dangers of inadequate timetable space for science and, on the shopfloor, standards are low partly because mathematical and scientific education in British schools is so poor. However, the two issues are considered as entirely distinct.

How do our neighbours fare in this key area? In West Germany some 30% of young people leave school at about sixteen with an intermediate certificate for which they are examined on an average of 10 subjects, including compulsory German, mathematics and a foreign language. Only 12% of English school-leavers reach such a level.

The average German standard for the lower half of the ability range is the same as the average for all English pupils. The average Japanese 13-year-old knows more mathematics than the average British 15-year-old. About 38% of Japanese 18-year-olds enter higher education; so do approximately 48% of North Americans. In Britain, that figure is 15%.

With regard to training, about 600,000 West German 18-year-olds embark annually on a three-year training course in industry and commerce leading to a vocational qualification. Between two and three times as many people qualify as fitters, electricians and building craftsmen as in Britain, and about five times as many clerical workers.

France, too, made considerable headway in the 1980s towards creating a vocationally qualified workforce capable of matching the Japanese and West Germans. The French train two to three times as many electricians and mechanics – more systematically and to higher standards – as the British through a system of vocational schools. By contrast, Britain relies on the two-year Youth Training Scheme. But the majority of young people who pass through it do not gain a vocational qualification, and of those who do, most gain only the basic qualifications available. (This may be because the YTS was initially designed as a job creation programme rather than as a course in vocational education.)

A survey by the Department of Employment's Training Agency found that half of all employees received no training in 1986-87. A third of employees said they had never received any training. A fifth of companies provided no training, less than one-third had a training budget and only 20% evaluated the effectiveness of training. There was a marked lack of enthusiasm for training among adults. More than half said they had no plans to undertake training in the future.

A recent report by the National Economic Development Office found that 63% of West German managers had a degree, and 51% of senior managers in the US had a second degree. Only 21% of British managers have a degree. One in five UK companies makes no provision for management training, rising to 75% among smaller companies.

Inadequate investment in education and training has contributed to the problem of a poorly skilled workforce. Improved training should help the labour market by equipping workers with the right kind and degree of skills to match job requirements. It should also gradually elevate the whole economy towards a higher level of skill, productivity and value-added production.

Too much of the British economy operates at a 'low skill equilibrium' with poorly skilled workers making products with a relatively low skill content. Training policy should move the economy towards a 'high skill equilibrium', where companies can innovate products and processes for growth markets with the benefit of more professional and adaptable workers.

How is it possible to move Britain up from its place near the bottom of the international training league table? Most employers and the government argue that a statutory training levy would be inefficient and bureaucratic. One writer has suggested that the problem is not simply one of funds but of culture: it is necessary to transform a culture based on energetic amateurism to one of constant professionalism. The debate is now wide open, but a swift and effective answer must be found if Britain is to meet the coming challenges.

Comprehension

1. What is the *skills shortage*?
2. Explain the phrase *to dull the country's competitive edge*.
3. What do you understand by *structural change*?
4. What are *shopfloor standards*? Why does the writer feel they are poor?
5. What are *fitters* and *building craftsmen*? List eight other common jobs that require vocational training.
6. Quote two criticisms of Youth Training Schemes.
7. Summarise in one sentence the findings of the report on managers' qualifications.
8. Explain the concepts of low and high skill equilibria.
9. What is a statutory training levy?
10. Why is the training problem perceived as a cultural phenomenon?

Links with Industry

1 Technology is becoming an increasingly crucial factor of competitiveness: industry must innovate more and more to compete in the global marketplace. Current estimates indicate that, although engineers are called on to perform tasks of growing complexity, their expertise has a lifetime of just four years!

One answer to the challenge lies in ever closer co-operation between industry and universities; educational establishments must be constantly aware of industry's precise needs, while industry must be aware of which specific fields of expertise are offered by establishments of higher education.

In an effort to shorten the discovery-teaching-application train, a joint US/European forum was launched in 1986 on the initiative of five companies. The participants examined the American National Technological University (NTU) scheme, which relies on a video and satellite network that allows universities to release sections of their best courses, which are picked up almost instantaneously by industries up and down the country.

However, the forum rejected the idea of extending NTU directly to Europe and sought to implement a scheme that is tailored to the European context.

What, then, is the role of industry in this two-way process? Broadly, business should input more into education and vice versa. Gary A. Frizell, education relations manager with Pacific Northwest Bell Telephone Company, declared: 'Business is the user of education's products – students – and it ought to replenish.' Companies should forge links with educational establishments to provide the highly specific training that new high-technology professions require. But many educationalists fear that there will be too many strings attached.

Political Footballs?

2 Politics are those processes of discourse through which members of society seek to assert and ultimately reconcile their wishes. So those people who wish to make education non-political are either failing to understand that the purposes and procedures of education are to reflect what people want, or they are trying, perhaps unconsciously, to restrict the rights of fellow citizens to participate in decisions of deep and abiding importance to them. In addition to individual objectives, education also has social objectives. It transmits the dominant culture to new generations.

The socialising process is implicit rather than overt in Britain. Its more specific components, though hard to find, can be discovered in those curiously mummified residues of established religion known as 'religious education' and the 'act of worship', which are the only elements imposed by law on the British curriculum. When they were written into the 1944 Education Act their authors must have had the same intentions as the Soviet educational planners who insisted on the teaching of compulsory Marxism.

from *The Politics of Educational Change* by Maurice Kogan

Interpretations in English — **Training for Life?**

Exercises

1. This text is very dense and rather difficult. Read the argument contained in the first paragraph. Rewrite the paragraph using three sentences and a total of between 40 and 45 words.

2. The education systems of most industrial countries are experiencing severe difficulties. To what are these due? Has the socialisation process changed in the past twenty years?

3. The writer mentions that religious education is the only compulsory subject in the British school curriculum and likens it to the teaching of Marxism in the Soviet Union. Give your reasons for agreeing or dissenting. Are there any compulsory subjects in your school system? If so, what are they? Compare your answers with a partner.

4. Organise a debate on one of the following motions

   'This house believes that compulsory religious education is useful in a modern-day school curriculum.'

   'This house believes that civilisation is the child of education.'

   'This house believes that a little knowledge is a dangerous thing.'

   'This house believes that ignorance is bliss.'

5. What are the specific features of the European context that would make it difficult to organise a scheme similar to the NTU? Make a list of the advantages and disadvantages of European co-operation. What technologies – if any – make it possible to circumvent any handicaps?

6. Make a list of ten products or professions that have emerged from the technological revolution of the latter part of this century (eg systems analysts, enterprise networks, fast food retailing).

7. One major problem of any Europe-wide scheme is that of language. Consider the following

   a) 2.4 billion people live in countries where English is used as a second language, 300 million speak it as a mother tongue, 300 million as a second language, and 1.8 billion have yet to learn it.

   b) One-third of the budget of the European Community's administration budget goes to pay for translation and interpretation.

   c) An editorial in *The Economist* newspaper stated that, in order to publish the final versions of key documents, the European Community had to make translations into each of its nine official languages. 'For all other purposes', the newspaper suggests, 'French and English should be enough'.

   Now turn to the grammar exercises on page 85.

Listening

Listen to the tape and answer the following questions

a) What does this conversation reveal about the employment landscape of Britain?

b) Talk with English people, if possible, or with people in your group and find out if there are any differences between the north and the south of the country.

c) What is the basic communication problem between these two people? Can education help get around those difficulties?

Training for Life? Interpretations in English

Discussion Points

* Choose a language or a language combination for a high-tech inter-European educational programme. What language or languages should be used by the European Community?

* The Chemical Bank of New York had to interview forty school-leavers from several different schools in order to find someone suitable to follow a training programme for clerks. The bank decided to adopt two of the schools and help form a debating league. Why?

* You are the Human Resources Manager for a company in one of the following sectors

    computer services
    consumer electronics
    financial services
    telecommunications
    pharmaceuticals

    You have been worried about the lack of specific training of school-leavers or university graduates. With a partner, devise three strategies involving link-ups with business and education to help overcome the problem.

* Governments tend to make alphabet soup when confronted with a problem! Find out from outside sources what organisations lie behind the following initials

MSC	*YTS*
ET	*CTC*
DTI	*LSE*
WEA	*NHS*

    Try and find some equivalent organisations from different countries.

Media Watch

Find a newspaper with job advertisements and circle those jobs that would suit your own qualifications and experience. Consider generally whether experience or qualifications seem the most important from the point of view of the advertisers.

Choose a job from a newspaper or magazine advert and, with a partner, prepare a short interview. Try and come up with questions and answers that could lead to you being offered a position in the company. Act out the roles in class.

Visit a Job Centre or similar facility and look at the advertisements on display. Note down the levels of qualifications required for some of the jobs on offer. Is there any evidence of information on training schemes? Choose three jobs of which you have some knowledge and make a comparative list. Choose another country of which you have some knowledge. Are the requirements higher, lower, or the same in that country?

Using the example opposite, fill in the other five job cards with similar information. Use examples from Britain, or your own country, or both for comparison.

Interpretations in English

Training for Life?

JOBCENTRE
- JOB: COOK
- DISTRICT: DIDSBURY
- PAY: £1-75 PER HOUR
- HOURS: 8.30 – 5.00 MON-FRI
- DETAILS: RESPONSIBLE FOR PREPARING EVENING MEALS + PACKED LUNCHES. SOME VEGETARIAN COOKING ESSENTIAL. OVERTIME AVAILABLE

ASK FOR JOB No. 143

JOBCENTRE
- JOB
- DISTRICT
- PAY
- HOURS
- DETAILS

ASK FOR JOB No.

JOBCENTRE
- JOB
- DISTRICT
- PAY
- HOURS
- DETAILS

ASK FOR JOB No.

JOBCENTRE
- JOB
- DISTRICT
- PAY
- HOURS
- DETAILS

ASK FOR JOB No.

JOBCENTRE
- JOB
- DISTRICT
- PAY
- HOURS
- DETAILS

ASK FOR JOB No.

JOBCENTRE
- JOB
- DISTRICT
- PAY
- HOURS
- DETAILS

ASK FOR JOB No.

unit nine

Questionnaire

A What are your ambitions? Map out your educational 'itinerary' (including what you intend to do) and compare it with those of other members of the class. Write down any differences that you notice, especially with reference to age and social background. Ask your teachers about their educational background.

B According to the information in the first text, other countries are more successful in their training effort than the UK. With a partner, write down all you can gather about training policies in a country of your choice (eg, the statutary levy of 1.1% of company wage bills in France; compulsory membership of chambers of commerce or trade in West Germany). Compare notes with groups who have covered different countries. Can you establish an 'international training league'?

C With your partner, find two strategies to improve the vocational training situation in Britain. Can you provide any suggestions for another country?

D Take a straw poll among the group and ask the question: 'Should business and education be closely linked?' What is the consensus? List the principal arguments for and against.

Afterthoughts

It is impossible for an Englishman to open his mouth without making other Englishmen hate or despise him.

George Bernard Shaw

A study by linguistics professor John Honey claims that accent differences still hamper social equality in Britain in the 1990s.

Should research necessarily have short term commercial applications in order to justify encouragement from government and society?

What is the difference, if any, between education and training? Given the choice, would it be better to have a well-educated or a well-trained population?

Tomorrow's World?

Tomorrow's World? — Interpretations in English

In the whole of Europe the only thing completely immune to the effects of acid rain is the British government.

* In 1979, only 27 of the thousands of beaches around Britain's coast were designated as safe for bathing.

Read the text and as you do so consider the following questions. Remember, you don't have to understand every word in order to answer them.

1. What is the main cause of pollution today?
2. Is anything being done to stop it?

A Dying Sea

Some of the most heavily polluted rivers in the world flow into the North Sea. The Rhine, for example, daily carries down from Europe's industrial heartland one hundred tons of toxic heavy metals, and it is the same story for the other six major rivers which discharge into the southern part of the North Sea: a deadly and never-ending flow of chlorines, acids and toxic metals.

Surprisingly, the River Thames now has a clean bill of health – an example of what can be achieved when the political will is there. It now has the cleanest metropolitan estuary in the world and salmon can be found swimming in it. However, one hundred miles to the north the Humber spews out a familiar brew of poisonous chemical compounds.

Occasional events bring the desperate plight of the North Sea to our attention. Most recently there has been an unprecedented growth in the quantity of marine algae using up vast amounts of the water's dissolved oxygen content, first killing fish and then the birds and seals which feed on them. The red tides of phytoplankton are created by another type of poison which is flowing into the North Sea at ever-increasing rates: the nitrates and phosphates which are used as fertilisers in intensive farming techniques and which are, sooner or later, washed off the agricultural land into the rivers. The North Sea suffers from airborne pollution, too; most of it carried eastward from Britain's coal and oil-fired power stations. The five million tons of sulphur and nitrogen oxides which belch from Britain's high chimneys each year fall either as acid rain over the Scandinavians (whose complaints are largely ignored) or fall into the North Sea. Britain refuses to go along with European attempts to limit such airborne pollutants. Other poisons are deliberately discharged into the skies above the North Sea by the three incinerator ships which are permanently moored 100 miles off the coast of Britain. There are many signs that the southern half of the North Sea, including the Wadden Sea, German Bight and the Jutland coast, is dying. Up to fifty per cent of certain types of fish caught in these waters are found to be diseased. A colony of seals living off the Dutch coast has shrunk from numbering 3000 to only 600 in a period of thirty years. In the space of one month during 1983, 30,000 sea birds were washed up on Scotland's eastern beaches; they had starved to death.

From time immemorial the North Sea has been a fertile source of fish for the fishing fleets of Europe and it still supports a population of some ten million sea birds. But its other and more recent role as rubbish tip for the industrial waste of Europe, is threatening to put an end to this. In the opinion of many, Britain deserves a large portion of the blame. 'Britain now stands isolated in vehemently defending its right to use coastal waters as a dumping ground for industrial waste,' says Greenpeace. Only time will tell whether public concern aroused by speeches from the Queen and the Prince of Wales can force a change in policy and thereby reduce the threat posed by the impending death of the North Sea.

Interpretations in English **Tomorrow's World?**

Comprehension

1. Why is the North Sea becoming so polluted?
2. What is surprising about the Thames today?
3. Why are the salmon so significant?
4. Using a dictionary if necessary, explain the phrase *spews out*.
5. Why are the seals in the North Sea threatened?
6. Give examples from the text of agricultural chemicals which are polluting the sea.
7. What is the problem with some of the chemicals discharged from British power stations?
8. In what sense is part of the North Sea 'dying'?
9. What is Britain's official attitude to the pollution of the North Sea?
10. What position has been taken by members of the British royal family?

Facing up to the Problem

1   A single disposal company, Intercontract SA of Fribourg, Switzerland, plans to dump 50,000 tons of chemical waste per year for ten years in the tiny West African state of Guinea-Bissau, which is no bigger than Wales. The French have been sending their toxic waste to Morocco for years.

       Toxic waste disposal is now big, international business in which a number of poor African nations have become embroiled. They charge less; it can cost as much as £280 per ton to dispose of toxic waste in Europe; in Africa it can cost less than two pounds. Even so, dumping payments can easily add up to two or even three times the national product of the countries concerned. The potential for bribery is immense. A London-based African diplomat claims to have been offered three million pounds as persuasion not to obstruct the settlement of a dumping contract. In 1988 a Norwegian consul was arrested in Guinea for forging documents required for dumping.

       According to the United Nations Environment Programme, dumping in Africa has increased as stricter anti-dumping laws are passed in industrialised countries and as other dump sites in the South Pacific and the Caribbean become filled. The only light at the end of the tunnel is that certain African countries have now made the dumping of some highly toxic substances illegal.

*   Explain how bribery and corruption are involved in the dumping business

2   Britain is the first European country to have to face up to the problem of where to put its radioactive waste. This is not just because Britain creates a large quantity of waste but because it has undertaken to process and dispose of the spent nuclear fuel from the atomic power stations of its European neighbours. This radioactive waste disposal business is worth about four hundred million pounds each year to the British economy. The irony is that the British still haven't decided how to make radioactive waste safe. So they have a temporary pile of nuclear rubbish which could fill the Palace of Westminster several times over. The most immediate problem concerns low and intermediate level waste products. The more highly radioactive waste cannot be permanently disposed of for at least fifty years anyway; it has first to cool down.

unit ten

Tomorrow's World?   Interpretations in English

There are two schools of thought on the problem of radioactive waste disposal; the first thinks the waste should be put somewhere, anywhere as far away as possible from population centres – perhaps in geologically fast tunnels miles beneath the surface of the earth or the seabed. The second (and these include the environmental lobby group Greenpeace) thinks the waste should be put somewhere where it can be monitored for leakage and where leaks, once established, are capable of being securely sealed. This seems by far the more responsible attitude, but the waste would have to be monitored for a hundred years or more and future generations may be less responsible than our own. In any case, do we have the right to impose this burden on them?

* Note down the main points of the two schools of thought on nuclear waste disposal.

3   HM Elizabeth II addresses King Olav of Norway at a banquet in his honour at Windsor Castle 12th April 1988

Seafaring is in the blood of both our peoples and the North Sea, which might appear to others as a barrier, has been a means of trade and communications and has provided natural resources for both our peoples for more than one thousand years. In more recent times we have co-operated to exploit its valuable oil and gas resources. It is therefore in the interests of both our nations to see that the health and cleanliness of the North Sea are maintained and that its renewable resources are only exploited on a sustainable basis.

* Explain the meaning of the last sentence in this speech.

Discussion Points

* Should a monarch make public statements on issues such as the environment?
* What should be done with the various levels of nuclear rubbish?
* Can poorer nations be protected from large scale pollution caused by international waste?

Now turn to the grammar exercises on page 86.

Listening

Listen to the recorded radio debate and then answer the following questions

* What are the main arguments put forward by John Mortimer in defence of the chemical industry?
* Does each step forward in progress always bring with it a new set of problems?

Language activity

Have a formal debate on one the following

'This house believes that some pollution is an inevitable concomitant of progress.'

'This house believes that a massive investment in nuclear power is the best way to reduce the greenhouse effect.'

'This house believes that economic growth threatens the well-being of the planet Earth and should no longer be an aim of government policy.'

'This house believes that nuclear power must remain as one of a range of energy sources but that substantial funds should be invested in alternative forms such as wind, tide and solar energy.'

Media Watch

Find some conservation/ecological journals and/or appropriate articles from newspapers and magazines and make a list of the current issues of concern. Make a list of pressure groups and organisations in Europe which call attention to environmental issues. Describe who they are and what they do.

Questionnaire

NIMBY is an acronym for an expression that has arisen to describe the way many people are prepared to protest only when policy decisions affect them personally. The letters stand for 'Not In My Back Yard'.

Prepare a suitable list of questions that will place interviewees in one of three categories

A Those who are pro-nuclear power but, as waste has to be disposed somewhere, would accept that it could have to be buried near them.

B Those who are pro-nuclear but unhappy about the storage of nuclear waste in the vicinity of their homes.

C Those who are anti-nuclear and believe that waste storage is a real and unresolved problem for everybody.

Present your results to the class.

Ask friends and acquaintances to

a) give you as many advantages and disadvantages of nuclear power as they can. Can you add any more?

b) give their understanding of the meaning of the term 'green'. Include your own definition.

Afterthought

Do we have the right, in the affluent and developed part of the world, to demand that countries less technologically advanced than our own should change their behaviour with regard to their own environment? Does the mounting of international economic pressure to twist the arms of an unwilling state amount to an unreasonable interference in a sovereign nation's internal affairs? Or is the urgency of our present predicament such as to justify any action that would help the global environment?

Perhaps we should reflect on how the colonialists of the past would have reacted had the indigenous population of a colony demanded that their natural resources should not be exploited because of the environmental consequences for the whole planet.

Interpretations in English **Grammar Exercises**

Grammar Exercises

Exercise A A group of English adjectives are formed by adding the suffix *-less* to certain nouns.

class*less* (= without class), penni*less* (= without money)

Choose an adjective ending in *-less* to go into the gaps below

Example *She told him it was ......**useless**...... to try any more.*

1 Europe is a .... society; whatever one's origins it is possible to rise up through the echelons.
2 The unemployed are .... to change society.
3 She was very .... to break three teacups.
4 He was a .... dictator who murdered thousands of people.
5 The climbing team was completely .... in the face of danger.
6 She was a .... worker; she did not stop till everything was finished.
7 Their business went bankrupt two years ago and they are now ....
8 We waited for hours to be rescued and began to think it was ....
9 The skier was .... in the face of the avalanche.
10 I get very angry when I see .... vandalism.

Exercise B Using a dictionary where required, fill the gaps below with suitable nouns.

1 That .... is quite brainless sometimes.
2 This .... should be painless.
3 This smokeless .... doesn't cause too much environmental pollution.
4 The hapless .... drove straight into a lamp post.
5 It was a fruitless .... I'm afraid.
6 The .... cleared the gate with an effortless jump.
7 The .... was somewhat featureless.
8 Unfortunately I found the .... to be rather humourless.
9 I'm not continuing in this thankless ....
10 He was a heartless .... and fully deserved his sentence.

A Question of Class

unit one 77

Grammar Exercises Interpretations in English

Exercise A Formal writing makes frequent use of passives.
Example *It is thought that women are unsuited to manual work.*

cf *Some people think that women are unsuited to manual work.*

If you need to keep the subject (here *some people*) it must become an object:

It is thought by some people that women are unsuited to manual work.

NB *Some people think* = verb in simple present

It is thought = to be plus past participle

Change the actives in the sentences below to passives where possible. Decide if you need to keep the subject to retain the sense.

1 Murdock argues that certain jobs are universally done by women. *It is argued*
2 Murdock maintains that men always do the hunting. *It is maintained*
3 In the Soviet Union women do most of the low paid jobs. *Most ... are done by*
4 Murdock argued that pregnancy was a handicap that weakened women. *It was argued*
5 A lot of people believe that having babies strengthens women. *It is believed*
6 You can assume that women do most of the housework in the Soviet Union. *It can be assumed*
7 In some cultures men and women share the heavy work. *The heavy work is shared*
8 Male caretakers always supervised the cleaners when I was at school. *The cleaners were always supervised*
9 A lot of people have noticed that in medicine men fill the highest positions. *It has been noticed ...*
10 The Equal Pay Act of 1975 removed only a certain amount of inequality. *Only — inequality was removed*

Exercise B Complete the following sentences using a passive form
Example In the USA, childcare *is still usually organised by women*

1 In Eastern Europe, the housework ....
2 In African cultures, work.................
3 In the 16th Century, trading ....
4 In the future, housework ....
5 In the 19th Century, girls ....
6 In an ideal world, work.................
7 In Murdock's opinion, labour ....
8· In my house, the boring jobs ....
9 In general, low-status work.................
10 In my opinion, labour ....

78 unit two

Interpretations in English — **Grammar Exercises**

Exercise A

In written English the phrase *took place* plus an adverbial can be used to express where or when something happened. This structure is favoured by journalists when they lack certain information. Replace the verbs in the sentences below with the related noun and use the phrase *took place*.

Example The British army shot three IRA men in Gibraltar.
The shooting took place in Gibraltar.

NB The original subject and object are dropped. It is no longer clear who shot whom.

1. The Contras killed seventeen farmers in the south of Managua.
2. The killer murdered his victim on the night of February 9th.
3. The members discussed the problem at the Annual General Meeting.
4. The Normans conquered England on September 28th, 1066.
5. A woman stabbed her husband in a council flat last month.
6. On thursday two taxi drivers argued for three hours outside a nightclub.
7. The Texan oil company drilled for oil seventy miles offshore.
8. In the past, English monarchs executed traitors in the Tower of London.
9. The management negotiated with the unions at a special meeting in Blackpool. (Make noun plural)
10. The theatre company performed before royalty at Stratford.

Exercise B

When expressing certain emotions in English it is sometimes possible to choose between the structure

a) subject + verb + object

and,

b) subject + *have* + noun phrase + *of/for* + object

Example a) I dislike apples.
b) *I have a dislike of apples.*

Change the sentences below to the simpler subject verb object structure (a). Where necessary, make adjectives into adverbs.

1. I have a dislike of cooking..............
2. He had a love of power..............
3. They have an absolute loathing for each other..............
4. She has a real liking for Italians..............
5. The youngsters had a deep distrust of authority..............
6. They should have an understanding of the situation..............
7. Those children had great respect for their parents..............
8. I have a strong suspicion of foul play..............
9. We don't have a fear of heights..............
10. Do you have a dread of failure?..............

unit three

Grammar Exercises   *Interpretations in English*

Exercise A   In English, *must not* (*mustn't*) is used when something is not allowed. *Need not* (*needn't*) is used when something is not necessary.

Fill in the appropriate word

1 You .... n't walk on the grass; they have planted bulbs there.
2 You .... n't walk on the grass; there's room on the pavement.
3 I .... n't stay up to see the film; I can easily video it.
4 I .... n't miss *Neighbours* today – it's the final episode!
5 You .... n't drink that, it's poison.
6 You .... n't drink it if you don't like it.
7 She .... n't forget her passport when she goes to the USA.
8 She .... n't take her passport when she goes to the Isle of Man.
9 You .... n't drive at 50 mph in a built-up area.
10 You .... n't drive fast; we aren't late.

Exercise B   When used affirmatively, *must* and *need to* are often interchangeable.
Finish the sentences below with an appropriate verb phrase.

1 When you take a lot of wine through customs you must..............................
2 If you want to buy stamps you need to ....
3 Anyone who visits Venice must..............................
4 If your passport's been stolen you need to..............................
5 If she intends to study at Oxford University she must ....
6 People who want to get *Sky* TV must..............................
7 Before one buys a house one usually needs to..............................
8 When you drive into a built-up area you must..............................
9 If you ride a motorbike in Britain you need to..............................
10 Before you can get antibiotics in Britain you must..............................

Interpretations in English **Grammar Exercises**

Exercise A

In English definitions can be made using relative clauses. Complete the following definitions using a relative clause introduced by *who* – for people and *which / that* – for things.

Example A consumer is *someone who buys products* ....

1 A manufacturer is ....
2 A product is ....
3 An adman is ....
4 A client is ....
5 The tease is ....
6 An advertising agency is ....
7 A billboard is ....
8 A market researcher is ....
9 Levi 501s are ....
10 Public Relations Officers are ....

Exercise B

The example below shows another possible use of relative clauses to make definitions. Complete the sentences below by filling in the gaps with *who, which* or *that*. Then choose a noun from the list below that fits the sentence.

Example A man or woman ..... *who* .... sells products for a company is called a .. *salesperson* ..

1 A product .... has no profit margin but attracts customers is called a ....
2 A person .... designs advertising ideas is sometimes called a ....
3 A persuasive talk .... is delivered by a salesperson is called a ....
4 An association .... monitors standards and infringements is known as a ....
5 A person .... lends out money at extortionate rates of interest is called a ....
6 A sales technique .... is particularly aggressive is known as the ....
7 The advertising style .... does not mention the name of the product is called the ....
8 Someone .... comes to your house uninvited to sell you something is called a ....
9 An accident .... involves a large number of fatalities is officially called a ....
10 A firm .... specialises in analysing the success of advertising campaigns is called a ....

*watchdog, sales pitch, disaster, loss leader
loan shark, visualiser, market research company
hard sell, tease, door-to-door salesman*

unit five   81

Grammar Exercises — *Interpretations in English*

Exercise A

Benjamin Weir had to go to the American Embassy *to get his passport renewed*. That is, another person (the Lebanese official) renewed his passport. Change and extend the phrases below to match this structure

1. Renew his work permit
   ....
2. Insure the car
   ....
3. Cut my hair
   ....
4. Value the house
   ....
5. Tune the piano
   ....
6. Dryclean the suit
   ....
7. Fix the television
   ....
8. Sign the letters
   ....
9. Cap this tooth
   ....
10. Transfer the cash
    ....

Exercise B

Put the following sentences into the simple past tense

Example   I get my passport renewed every year ... *I got my passport renewed every year*

1. I get my work permit renewed every year ....
2. I have to get the car serviced ....
3. She is thinking about getting the ring valued ....
4. They want to get the roof seen to as soon as possible ....
5. She gets her hair permed at Gino's ....
6. He wants to get his glasses mended ....
7. He is considering getting the loft insulated ....
8. I'll be getting my visa extended at the consulate ....
9. Will she be able to get the dress altered? ....
10. I'll get my wheel clamped for illegal parking ....

Interpretations in English **Grammar Exercises**

Exercise A It is sometimes difficult to decide when to use *quite* or *rather*. *Quite* usually means less than 'very', but with certain adjectives it can mean 'completely'. *Rather* also means less than 'very', but is more often associated with adjectives that are negative in their meaning.

Examples *She's quite good at maths, she came fourth in her class.*
She's rather weak at spelling.
I'm quite sure I recognise him.

Fill in the correct word (*quite / rather*) in the sentences below

1 He's .... intelligent, but he can't concentrate.
2 She's .... untidy I'm afraid.
3 I'm .... certain you never told me.
4 She's .... fast at typing, but her shorthand is .... slow.
5 It's .... true; I've forgotten.
6 It's a nice house, ... well decorated though it's in a .... noisy neighbourhood.
7 I'm .... disappointed in the car, to be honest.
8 I'm always .... hesitant when I drive in France and I find the centre of Paris .... impossible.
9 I thought he looked .... attractive but his conversation turned out to be .... boring.
10 My children are getting .... too good at saying what they think.

Exercise B *Somewhat* is used in a similar way to *rather*. *absolutely* means *completely*.

Complete the sentences below with suitable adjectives

1 She thinks the concept of unilateral disarmament is rather ....
2 As a military power, the USSR has always been quite...
3 To a lot of people, the concept of nuclear war is absolutely ....
4 The old-style conventional warfare was quite ....
5 Nowadays most people think a war between USA and USSR is somewhat ....
6 The amount of money spent on weapons is quite ....
7 The recent talks between USSR and USA have been very ....
8 The idea of third world countries holding nuclear weapons is rather...
9 Many people think pacifists are somewhat...
10 To others, the pacifists are quite ....

unit seven

Grammar Exercises   *Interpretations in English*

Exercise A   Complete the sentences below with a suitable preposition
1   I'm afraid I don't share your interest .... computer programming.
2   Computers are now indispensible. The reason .... this is their accuracy and speed .... operation.
3   Computers do not have the solution .... most management problems.
4   This mainframe can make contact .... other terminals all .... the world.
5   There is no direct link .... my micro and his workstation.
6   Hal could reply .... any of the crew's questions .... normal English.
7   There has been a fall .... the cost .... software recently.
8   Your reasons .... learning .... writing programs are quite different .... mine.
9   There is a lot of difference .... ASSEMBLY and COBOL.
10 There is a huge difference .... price .... the Amstrad and the IBM.

Exercise B   Complete the following sentences with a preposition from the list below and add a suitable noun phrase
1   I'm interested ....
2   I spend it all ....
3   All the fuss was ....
4   He is staying..
5   She is staying ....
6   I've just got up ....
7   Can you get it finished ....
8   My friend works...
9   He's working..
10 They're employed ....

in, under, by, for, to, at, over, on, by

Interpretations in English **Grammar Exercises**

Exercise A The form *used to* is used in English to talk about a past habit that does not happen anymore. It often refers to fairly distant past time. Complete the sentences below saying what used to happen as well using the noun in brackets.

Example *They still have archery classes at my old school (FENCING)*
They used to have fencing classes as well

1 They still play hockey at the grammar school (LACROSSE)

2 I still watch schools TV even though my children have grown up (CHILDREN'S HOUR)

3 The boys still have to wear blazers at St Josephs (CAPS)

4 You still need a modern language to read linguistics at that university (LATIN)

5 A lot of girls still have to learn cookery at school (NEEDLEWORK AND IRONING)

6 In the village nursery school they still read them Grimm's fairytales (THE BIBLE)

7 Young people can still claim the dole on that training course (TRAINING ALLOWANCE)

8 You can still do German in the local adult education college (SPANISH)

9 People usually need maths GCSE to study chemistry at university (GERMAN)

10 You still get valuable experience on the YTS programme (JOB)

Exercise B Finish the sentences below

1 My son used to be enthusiastic about school but now ....

2 The youngsters used to expect to get a job at the end of a youth training programme but now ....

3 There used to be corporal punishment in most British schools but now

4 Teachers used to be drawn almost exclusively from the middle classes but now

5 Careers Officers used to offer a wide range of job possibilities but now

6 It used to be easy to go and work in, say, Australia but now

7 You used to see dozens of jobs advertised in the Job Centres but now

8 There used to be a religious service every day in almost all schools but now

9 Most British schools used to insist on a strict uniform but now

10 I used to tell the children: 'Your schooldays are the best days of your life', but now

unit nine

Grammar Exercises

Interpretations in English

Exercise A

A common conditional form in English is one that predicts that if one event takes place, another will follow. In such conditionals, reference to future time is made in the main clause, although in the subordinate *(if)* clause the simple present is used.

Example *If the river gets too dirty the salmon will disappear.*

Complete the follow conditional sentences using the verbs indicated.

1. If the sea gets too polluted the fish .... *(die)*
2. If too many nitrates are allowed to flow into the sea the phytoplankton .... *(increase)*
3. If the Queen feels strongly about the latest report she .... *(speak out)*
4. If the sea is too badly poisoned it .... *(recover)*
5. If action is taken immediately the sea .... *(die)*
6. If the Humber is cleaned up the number of fish .... *(can increase)*
7. If the Avon gets too polluted most of its fish .... *(can survive)*
8. If the North Sea is not rescued soon the fishermen .... *(can survive)*
9. If European governments act fast the situation .... *(get worse)*
10. If the British government continues to ignore the problem the situation .... *(can be reversed)*

Exercise B

In informal English, a similar construction may be used where the subordinate clause is introduced by *once*. There is somewhat less doubt expressed that the event is going to happen than in conditionals beginning with *if*, and the form may be used in the sense of a warning or reassurance:

Example Once he discovers that delicatessen *he'll stop going to the supermarket*

Complete the following sentences

1. Once she tries that wine ....
2. Once they start arguing ....
3. Once he starts crawling ....
4. Once we get settled into our flat ....
5. Once he realizes they are married ....
6. Once you start driving to work ....
7. Once they know you're leaving ....
8. Once she learns to open the door ....
9. Once they get on television ....
10. Once you get used to it ....

Interpretations in English   Tape Transcripts

Listening: Tape Transcripts

A Question of Class

During a visit to London, a tourist is discussing British newspapers with an English acquaintance over a pub lunch.

Tourist I hear that more newspapers are sold in Britain than anywhere else in the world. Is that true?

Man Yes. I can think of at least eight papers that a lot of people buy.

Tourist I know *The Times*. Do you read that?

Man Oh no! That's a posh paper read by people who rule the country.

Tourist On the bus I noticed a man reading the *Daily Mirror*.

Man Oh, that's read by the people who think they run the country.

Tourist Is it communist?

Man No. The *Morning Star* is the one that's read by the people who think the country ought to be run by another country.

Tourist What's that pink newspaper he's reading?

Man That's the *Financial Times,* read by the people who own the country – and the bloke next to him reading *The Guardian* probably thinks he ought to be running the country.

Tourist So what other papers are there?

Man Well, there's the *Daily Mail* – that's read by the wives of the people who run the country. Then there's the *Daily Express* which is read by the people who think the country ought to be run as it used to be run.

Tourist That's terrible.

Man Yes, but the people who read *The Daily Telegraph* think it still is!

Tourist My English teacher says there's a paper called *The Sun* which is like a comic.

Man Yes. That's read by the people who don't care who runs the bloody country providing the page three girls don't go away. Right now, what are you drinking?

Housewives' Choice?

Presenter And now at two minutes past two, it's time for Female Focus presented by Jenny Parkes.

JP Hello. If you're a housewife do you consider yourself to be a second class, even a second-rate citizen, tied to menial tasks such as changing nappies and cleaning the loo, unrepresented, unpaid and unloved? Or do you see the housewife's role as a vital mainspring of society – perhaps you prefer to call yourself a Domestic Manager or a House Secretary? Well, in the studio today we welcome Anne Morris, Labour MP for Winnington, Manchester, who has just published her controversial book *Housewife Equals Slave*, and Baroness Hawkes, author, former marriage guidance counsellor and member of the House of Lords. Can I turn first to you, Anne. Why do you see a housewife as a slave?

Listening   87

AM Well first of all, status. Or lack of it. No job I can think of commands less respect than the occupation of wife and mother. It goes completely unrecognised and usually unthanked. Then there's the pay. Mostly, housewives get little or no pay in return for the hours put in which are terribly long, sometimes virtually twenty-four hours a day, and of course the work itself is physically and mentally draining. I can't think of any man who would work quite as hard with no pay, no power, or any other reward at the end of it.

BH Now come on. The power you have is surely the influence you have on your children's lives, on your husband's life – to bring up a happy, healthy family is surely the most fulfilling job one could ask for. I agree being a housewife is a demanding job, but in no other job can you see the fruits of your labour so clearly: that is, contented, well-balanced children.

JP Anne Morris, surely you aren't putting down the work done by women at home; I mean why is say, working in a factory any better?

AM Working in a factory isn't always better. Actually, I think too many women do too many of the more repetitive factory jobs – the thing is women factory workers often run the house as well after they've finished work – but at least they are paid and recognised for work outside the home.

BH But this is exactly my point. If women stuck to house management and the man was responsible for going out and earning the salary, then the wife would not be so exhausted and would have time for the children who will otherwise, as we know, become vandals and drug addicts and so on. Someone has to take proper care of the family or the family and society suffer.

JP Anne Morris, a final word?

AM I think that for too long women have remained isolated and unrewarded in their role as housewives and I think their hard work should be paid for by society. I don't think all the responsibility for happy families lies with women and the sooner men start to share both the high status positions and the dirty jobs the better.

JP Anne Morris, Baroness Hawkes, thank you very much.

The Fourth Estate

The following is a conversation between the editor, assistant editor, news editor and advertising sales manager of a typical British newspaper

Ed So, what are we leading with in the first edition?

Ass Well, we've got a choice: there's a Royals story; apparently Princess Di doesn't like the food they're giving them on the royal tour in Australia.

Ed Mmm, Di Slams Aussie Tucker! Not bad. That's a possibility. What have you got, Mary?

News Well, that vice story is breaking – you remember, prominent peer seen in West End massage parlour.

Ed: Oh yes... Lord erm Whatsisname.

News That's right. Tory peer. We've got the photos now, too. We paid the girl twenty thousand quid for that little lot, so it'll be a pity not to go ahead with it.

Ed	Publish and be damned eh? Well, we'll have to do the usual round of interviews – shocked wife, indignant politicos at Conservative Central Office, you know, the usual thing.
Ass	Don't forget the Press Council is coming down heavily against invasion of privacy these days.
Ed	Ha, the Press Council! Paper tigers!
News	That's right. And don't forget our readers. We've got over two million readers who say we've got it right.
Ed	No, that's a strong possibility for page one. Talking of politicos, any political stories, John?
Ass	Yes, apparently a Cabinet Minister's wife was stopped for speeding last night. Turns out she was well over the limit – a hundred milligrams or something.
News	Great!
Ass	And that's not all. Apparently the husband said she was unlucky to be caught.
News	Lucky not to have got herself killed!
Ed	Or killed some other poor bastard! Okay John, pursue that one. Any disasters?
News	Well, that little boy from Manchester – the one with the new heart. He's holding on but doctors don't expect him to survive the night. We've got a team of reporters and photographers at the hospital and outside the parents' home for when death occurs.
Ed	Right. Any sporting news today?
Ass	Not really. There are rumours of sex and drugs at a party given for the England cricket team in the West Indies. We are in touch with a hotel porter in Kingston, but nothing definite yet.
Ed	Yes, be careful with the facts on that one, John. It can be terribly embarrassing if we get things wrong. I still can't show myself in the wine bar after that last cock-up: 'I slept with peer's ghost!' – then the peer shows up alive and kicking and proceeds to sue us! Very inconvenient! Finally, is the advertising Sales Manager here – oh yes. Now I'm not happy about that lingerie ad on page five; the girl is almost naked. We can't have that, you know, we are a family newspaper after all.

Television is Watching You!

The following discussion is from an imaginary radio programme concerning the future shape of current affairs in TV in the light of government censorship, pressure to compete for advertising and the threat from satellite broadcasting.

At the heart of the discussion is the concept of *Infortainment* – a new form of current affairs, based on American-style formats, that relies on feature journalism. This child of our times argues that conventional current affairs will only be watched if injected with a strong dose of show business techniques. It doesn't show what's really going on in the world. Infortainment is entertaining but notable for what it will not tackle: few investigations into political or commercial corruption and a propensity to take the easy option.

James is an editor of uncompromising current affairs and news programmes. The other speaker, Rachel, is a producer of an 'infortainment' type current affairs programme. We join the debate with James defending traditional investigative current affairs against the charge that it is somehow a protected species and unconcerned with popular appeal.

James	Take the centre-piece of our current affairs output *This Week This World*, for example. It is subject to forceful criticism. We are keenly aware of our audience and aware of the constant pressure we're under. To deny this and to imply we're not preoccupied with our audience, actual and potential, or to claim we don't covet popularity, is to fly in the face of the facts. It is true, however, that we are not afraid of upsetting people, and if we stopped doing that then I believe we would not be meeting our responsibilities.
Rachel	You seem to be suggesting that your aim is to be both popular and unpopular at the same time. This seems like a contradiction.
James	Well, yes. It's important to tackle things that, in many ways, are unpopular. If we decide to make a programme about Nicaragua, or indeed Afghanistan, there will inevitably be a drop in the viewing figures. It would be wrong to treat such subjects in a superficial way. They warrant in-depth, extended coverage and it is an accepted fact that a large segment of the public have a very short span of concentration. But should we back away from dealing with these subject areas? The danger is that with fewer programmes of this kind, fewer people will have the interest or capacity to watch them.
Rachel	Yes, but we also deal with difficult and challenging subjects. The concerns of ordinary people, such as should we buy eggs or chicken produced under certain conditions, is it safe to fly in a plane manufactured by Boeing, are the channel ferries safe and so on. These are difficult topics and ones which we are prepared to take on from week to week. You are up against powerful vested interests, government departments, you know, our programmes are important too.
James	Fine. But you can't have a safe and unremitting diet, as it were, of consumer issues and you surely have a duty to bring to the public something unexpected, provocative or even unsettling.
Presenter	Documentaries involving a lot of painstaking investigative work are very expensive though, aren't they?
James	This is the issue. We don't want to disappear through financial cutbacks, censorship or pressure from advertisers to appeal to a particular sector of their market. Rachel's programme is high quality television too, there's room for more than one kind of approach to current affairs. But we must resist all pressures to limit the scope of journalists; I mean, there seems to be an unwritten law never to mention Northern Ireland.
Rachel	But I think we're on the same side. I'm under pressure too. Most people in television are worried about the possible auctioning of franchises and political pressure from whatever quarter.
Presenter	How do you see the future of current affairs television then, James?
James	I am genuinely afraid that programmes catering for large minority interests, like foreign language broadcasts, highbrow arts items, religious affairs and investigative documentaries will give way to tabloid TV. And this is already beginning to happen. We are fast approaching a situation where advertisers will decide what we can watch and what we can't.
Presenter	So everything would be dictated by ratings and restricted by costs tending towards mediocre quality, cheap American films and soaps, for example, with very little room for serious drama?
James	Yes; and the high quality television that we are all justly proud of will be under threat.

Rachel   I don't agree that quality will inevitably suffer, though I do think we could end up with far less choice than we enjoy at the moment. It would be a tragedy if programmes like ours became too expensive to make.

Presenter   Well, we seem to have reached a consensus and at this point I must thank Rachel Grade and James Morissey for coming on the programme and remind listeners that there will be an opportunity to phone in with your comments on what has been said during this programme at midday tomorrow when your host on *Radio Listens* will be Jennifer Roberts. Goodbye.

Soft Sell

The advertising executive and his client are having a preliminary discussion about how best to project the new product: the CBX 550.

A   Hello, come in and may I say how pleased we are at Absell that you have decided to give us your account. Now the CBX 550 – a wonderful product.

C   Ah, thank you. We're all very pleased with it at the factory...

A   Yes, a beautiful machine. We'll have no trouble thinking up some sales support – as we like to call it – for the CBX 550.

C   Oh good. We're all very proud of the CBX at John Cole and Son. We're a small company you know and it's important this product sells well.

A   Sexy.

C   I beg your pardon?

A   Sexy – I think that should be our approach. Let's see now, we could have... (I'm thinking of billboards) ...now we could have a picture of a young chap, wearing a crash helmet, leathers, boots, the works, surrounded by female admirers with the slogan 'Imagine yourself astride the CBX: it could change your life' – something like that.

C   No, I don't think that kind of approach would work. That wouldn't do at all.

A   No, no, perhaps not. We could blind them with science: 'At the heart of the 550 is a new high-tech engine; multi-valve power with the intelligence of a computer to control ignition and fuel mix...' You know the sort of thing.

C   Yes, but the CBX 550 doesn't have a computer controlled ignition or fuel mix. Sorry.

A   Never mind; I've got it. We've got to appeal to the consumer's sense of belonging – you know, something like: 'Have you noticed who is using the CBX 550? Don't you deserve the new CBX 550?'. We could get a famous personality to say he or she owns one.

C   I'm not convinced that would be the best approach.

A   No? Well we could go for the straight, no nonsense approach, targeting the sophisticated yuppy who is always on the go, always in a hurry, you know: 'With a lifestyle like yours how long can you be without the new CBX 550?'

C   I'm afraid we don't get many yuppies among our usual clients; no, I'm quite sure that approach won't work.

A   No, perhaps not. We could always try and appeal to the commuter. That's a very large market these days you know.

C   The commuter? But...

A	How about a picture of queues of cars with the new CBX 550 overtaking the whole lot, a slogan like: 'Say goodbye to traffic jams. On the new CBX 550 you'll be as free as the wind.'
C	Mr Adams, I think you've got the wrong idea about John Cole and Son – and our new product.
A	Nonsense, I used to ride a motorcycle myself when I was a lad.
C	A motorcycle? But Mr Adams, the CBX 550 is a tractor. We make agricultural machinery.
A	A tractor! Good God. Oh well, we could always try humour. Something like: 'Have you ever tried to plough a field with a motorbike? Try the new CBX 550 instead.'
C	No, Mr Adams, I still don't think you understand...

Murderers or Martyrs?

In May 1984 American Presbyterian Missionary Benjamin Weir, a veteran of 31 years in the Lebanon was taken hostage. He spent sixteen months in captivity and on his release started to write a book about the experience. The book is called *Hostage Bound, Hostage Free*. In it he includes some of the conversations he had with his captors, members of the Islamic Jihad (*Islamic Holy War*) group. Here is one, from the early days of captivity; two of his captors have come to question him and the second asks him for his name

BW	Benjamin Weir. I'm a pastor.
C2	What pastor?
BW	Pastor is a minister, serving a church. I'm a Protestant – Injili.
C2	What church?
BW	Protestant church. Lebanese church. National Evangelical Synod of Syria and Lebanon.
C1	You Catholic?
BW	No, Protestant. I also teach.
C1	What you teach?
BW	I teach at the Near East School of Theology sometimes.
C2	What theology?
BW	Theology is studying about God.
C2	Oh, you priest?
BW	Well, not exactly, but like a priest. I'm a pastor.
C2	Okay. You American?
BW	Yes, I'm an American.
C2	We know you work with the American Embassy.
BW	No, that's not true. I have nothing to do with the American Embassy.
C1	But we know you go there.
BW	Yes, I go to get my passport renewed when necessary, but I don't work with the Embassy.
C2	Who do you know at the Embassy?

BW	Well, I know the Lebanese man in the consular section who renewed my passport.
C2	Who else do you know?
BW	I don't know anyone else. I'm not even sure who the ambassador is now.
C2	We know you work with the Embassy.
BW	You are wrong! I have no political connections.
C2	Maybe you don't work at the Embassy, but we know you are a spiritual advisor.
BW	My friend, that's not true. You don't know much about the US government if you think they have spiritual advisors. I'm not connected with the Embassy in any way.
C2	We will give you time to think about the people you know at the Embassy. I'll be back to get the names from you.
BW	I don't need time because I don't know anyone there. I'm telling you the truth.
C2	We will be back later. For sure you know the names.

With that parting remark the two men went out, leaving me in a quandary. How could I answer what I didn't know?

After lunch – another sandwich, this time canned tuna with slices of pickle and a can of Pepsi Cola – the two interrogators returned.

C1	How are you?
BW	Okay.
C1	What do you need? Aspro? Medicine?
BW	No, I'm okay. But I think I have an eye infection. Last time the doctor told me to use Terramycin eye ointment. Can you get some Terramycin eye ointment – a salve? You know, in a tube, for my eyes?
C2	Terramycin. We'll see.
BW	And a Bible – the Injil. Holy Book. I need to read the Bible.
C2	We'll see. Tell us now the names of people you know at the American Embassy.
BW	I told you, I don't know any. No matter how many times you ask, I don't know people there.
C2	Well, you think about it and let us know.

By the end of his captivity, Benjamin Weir's questioners were bringing the book *English for Beginners* into the interrogations with them and treating the sessions as English lessons.

Defence of the Realm

A civil servant working in the Ministry of Defence has leaked a document to Opposition MPs. At Prime Minister's Question Time in the House of Commons, the Shadow Defence Secretary rises to speak

SD	Is the Prime Minister aware of the shocking – I must even say abominable – contents of this report from the Ministry of Defence? It is the ultimate proof of the utter immorality of the military-industrial complex in general and of this government in particular.
PM	I'm afraid I am unaware of what the Right Honourable gentleman is talking about – if indeed he is talking about anything of substance.

SD	Prime Minister, I am talking about Nato's plan to start a war with the Warsaw Pact.
	(Voice of Speaker: 'Order, order...')
PM	I hope the Right Honourable Gentleman realises the import of what he is saying.
SD	I hope the Prime Minister is aware of his share of the responsibility for starting World War Three! Allow me to quote from the foreword to the document: 'In view of the massive superiority of the Warsaw Pact conventional forces and the unexpected success of recent Soviet diplomacy in persuading certain front-line European countries to disarm or to refuse the siting of nuclear weapons on their soil, the only viable way of containing the communist advance is by means of a limited nuclear strike by Nato forces.
Speaker	I hope that the Right Honourable Gentleman has some means of substantiating these outrageous claims! He knows perfectly well that Nato is a defensive alliance.
SD	I am also aware of the Secretary of Defence's recent claim that all weapons are defensive and all spare parts non-lethal. Allow me to continue: 'Such a strike would never, under normal circumstances, be tolerated by public opinion (although all member governments agree as to the danger of the Soviet advance). We therefore recommend that a nuclear device of a type used by the Warsaw Pact be exploded at the US army base at Frankfurt, West Germany. Casualties will regrettably be heavy but this would allow us to take advantage of the shock effect to launch our own strike on Warsaw Pact tank units based in East Germany and Poland, thereby gaining a vital strategic advantage.'
PM	The Right Honourable Gentleman is either a knave or a total and utter fool. He is the victim of an elaborate hoax. ('Hear, hear' etc) It is unthinkable that any Western power – and especially any Nato member – would attack another country, whatever the circumstances. That is why we have a Ministry of Defence and not a Ministry of War!

This is I.T.!

Perhaps one of the most brilliant portrayals of a computer was created by Stanley Kubrick in his film of the mid nineteen sixties entitled *2001: A Space Odyssey* which was based on the novel by Arthur C. Clarke. The mystery of man, man-made intelligence and a transcendent intelligence is explored but, unsurprisingly, not explained. The problematic relationship between man and machine is highlighted in another episode of Dr Frankenstein and the Monster. The computer is called Hal and malfunctions at a critical point during the mission to Jupiter. The voyage was begun in an attempt to find the secret of a strange object – obviously created by intelligent life – discovered beneath the surface of the moon. This monolithic artifact emitted a strong signal directly towards the planet Jupiter. The most advanced computer to have been constructed, which had never been known to make a mistake, was in charge of the mission.

However, this summit of man's achievement fails at the critical moment but events are taken over by a higher unseen intelligence and the protagonists reach their goal in spite of the failure of mere human technology. In a moving scene, the hero switches off the computer in a bid to save the mission and the layers of Hal's intelligence are unpeeled and discarded like an onion as, one by one, the modules of its 'brain' are removed. The death of the computer has the same emotional charge as if the film was dealing with the demise of a sympathetic human character. The computer begs him to stop and reduced to the capacity of an infant sings a nursery rhyme that evidently played a part in the programming/training of the machine. Hal says at one point: 'I can feel my mind going...'.

The dialogue that follows takes place after the crew (Dave and Frank) first suspect that all is not well with the computer that they and the mission are relying on.

Dave	Well Hal, I'm damned if I can find anything wrong with it.
H	Yes; it's puzzling, I don't think I've ever seen anything quite like this before. I would recommend that we put the unit back in operation and let it fail. It should then be a simple matter to track down the cause. We can certainly afford to be out of communication for the short time it will take to replace it.
Mission Control	Xray Delta One, this is Mission Control, Roger, you're 1930. We confer with your plan to replace number one unit to check fault prediction. We should advise you, however, that our preliminary findings indicate that your onboard 9000 computer is in error predicting the fault. I repeat, in error predicting the fault. I know this sounds rather incredible, but this conclusion is based on results from our twin 9000 computer. We are sceptical ourselves and we are running cross-checking routines to determine the reliability of this conclusion. Sorry about this little snag, fellas, we'll get this info to you just as soon as we work it out. Xray Delta One this is Mission Control 2049 transmission concluded.
H	I hope the two of you are not concerned about this.
Dave	No; we're not.
H	Are you quite sure?
Dave	Yes. I'd like to ask you a question though.
H	Of course.
Dave	How would you account for this discrepancy between you and the twin 9000?
H	Well, I don't think there's any question about it. It can only be attributable to human error.
Frank	Listen Hal, there's never been any incidence at all of a computer error occurring in the 9000 series, has there?
H	None whatsoever, Frank; the 9000 series has a perfect operational record.
Frank	Well of course I know all the wonderful achievements of the 9000 series but are you certain there's never been any case of even the most insignificant computer error?
H	None whatsoever. Frank, quite honestly I wouldn't worry myself about that.
Dave	Well I'm sure you're right, Hal. Fine. Thanks very much. Oh Frank, I'm having a bit of trouble with my transmitter in C pod, I wonder if you'd come down and take a look at it with me?
Frank	Yes.
Dave	See you later, Hal.

Training for Life?

Darrel is nineteen. He has left school – an inner-city comprehensive in the north west of England – with no formal qualifications, like many of his classmates. Some of his friends have found unskilled jobs and have become wage-earners, others are collecting unemployment benefit. Two have joined government-sponsored training schemes.

Darrel has been offered a job driving a van for a local food company, for which he will earn £120 per week. He still lives with his parents: his mother is a housewife and his father is unemployed. He meets his old school Careers Officer in town who encourages Darrel to join the Youth Training Scheme and pick up some basic skills in data processing.

Tape Transcripts
Interpretations in English

CO   You're not going to take that job with Smithwick's, are you?

D   And why not? It's good money and I'm more or less my own boss.

CO   But it won't get you anywhere. You've got a good brain, you know. Why not use it? You were pretty good at maths at school. Take a course with the YTS and get yourself a qualification.

D   What good will that do me? Look at my dad. He's a qualified fitter and he's been on the dole for three years. Fat lot of good a qualification did him!

CO   I know, but times have changed. Your dad works in what they call the 'twilight industries', you know, like shipbuilding and steel. Times have changed. If you get yourself a grounding in computers, you'll be able to do what you want. Move out of this place for a start!

D   Oh yeah? Where to? The only place you can find work is down south, and they're all snobs down there. They'd take the micky out of my accent for a start. I know, 'cause that's what happened to my mate Derek.

CO   Oh come off it. It's not like that. There's lots of opportunities... and that's where the jobs are.

D   Sure. But where would I live? Derek flogged his house, you know, one of those terraced ones in Garton Street, for fifteen grand. You know how much the same thing cost in Portsmouth? Fifty thousand! He had to travel up and down at the weekend and live with his Mum and Dad!

CO   But you earn better money to pay for that. You must look at training as the key to your future. It might be hard at first, but once you've got your qualification, you're laughing.

D   And what do I do in the meantime? I've seen how much them apprentices are paid. It's only ten quid more than the dole. I'd rather draw unemployment and do nowt. At least with £120 I can buy myself some decent clothes and go out for a pint when I feel like it.

CO   I don't think you realise what's at stake.

D   Now you're talking posh, just like they do on the telly when they talk about them schemes. No ta, I'm better off driving a van. At least there'll be one pay packet in the house.

Tomorrow's World?

Announcer   Hello and welcome to *Our World*. Tonight in the studio we have Andy Pearson of the environmental pressure group Worldwatch and John Mortimer of the Chemical Industries Association. The question we are all pondering tonight is: how can we put a stop to the pollution that threatens our country? First, Andy:

AP   Well, first of all, it's not just our country that's at risk but the seas that surround it and the air that we breathe above it. All these elements are finite and we have to try and persuade the chemical industry that...

JM   That's all very well but do you intend to legislate to stop people using certain products or driving their cars? Everybody has the right to choose how they live... the sort of lifestyle they wish to pursue. The lifestyle we enjoy today would have been unthinkable only thirty years ago. May I ask you how you travelled to the studio this evening? Did you walk or ride a bicycle?

AP I drove here. But I made sure the car I was driving was using unleaded petrol. If I have a choice I always try to minimise environmental damage and I believe most people, if they stopped to think, would do the same. Ten years ago it was only possible to buy leaded petrol. Now the oil companies are offering us the choice. And, if I may go on for a second, it's interesting that John refers to our lifestyle thirty years ago because 1956 was the year that parliament passed the Clean Air Act. That was necessary because air pollution was killing hundreds of people every year. Now that Act cut down on the use of untreated coal for heat and power and thereby improved our lifestyle in a very important way. Also, it obviously did not have a drastic effect on economic development.

JM OK. Let's look at one area where there can be no doubting the contribution of the chemical industry to the good life... or any sort of life; life full-stop: medicines. Now, my son is asthmatic. He has trouble with breathing. He's had it since he was a boy. But you would hardly notice from talking with him. There are medicines available today which enable him to live a completely normal life – if you can call canoeing and mountaineering and scuba-diving leading an ordinary life! Now I don't need to remind you that medicines are chemicals, they start a chemical reaction in the body...

AP Let's pursue that a little further. Asthma, the figures tell us, is on the increase. In fact it's of the order of ten times more common now than it was two generations ago... say fifty years ago. Now, we don't really understand asthma – or any of the other allergic reactions, but your son and all other asthmatics are responding to something in the air. And the only thing that has changed the air in the last fifty years is industrial pollution. There's probably less plant pollen, if anything. So it may very well be that modern medicines, admirable though they are, are doing no more than putting right the problems – the unnecessary problems in our view – of modern life. Look at food and fertilisers; another case in point where over-production has led to damage of the environment and the economic disasters of the EEC food mountains for instance...

JM But look at the extensive range in vegetables and fruit that can be bought at every high street supermarket today. Thanks to chemical preservatives you can eat most produce all the year round. If you want to recall how things used to be, go to China in winter time and you'll be on a limited diet of tinned mushrooms and cabbage!

AP Yes, but can you deny that the unrestricted use of phosphates and nitrates is having a terrible effect on our environment? They get into our rivers and into our seas killing off the fish. And the effect on the farms themselves, chemicals are killing off our wild flowers and the insects on which our birdlife feeds. Instead we're breeding a strain of super-bugs which are impervious to all pesticides unless these are administered in larger and larger doses. And why are we doing all this intensive farming? To cut down on manpower – so we can produce more for less. And in the meantime agriculture workers are being laid off, rural communities are being destroyed and villages are becoming the haunts of yuppies.

JM Now hold your horses. You can't stop people from...

AP I don't want to stop people from doing what they want, but we have to try and educate the consumer and the industrialist alike. We can have the good life, with a pollution-free environment, but there has to be the political will and public concern must be fostered in order to bring pressure to bear on the policy makers before it's too late. Consider the depletion of the ozone layer and the contribution this makes to the greenhouse effect; again it is chemicals contained in aerosols that are to blame.

Grammar Exercises: Keys

A Question of Class

Exercise A

1 Europe is a classless society; whatever one's origins it is possible to rise up through the echelons.
2 The unemployed are powerless to change society.
3 She was very careless to break three teacups.
4 He was a ruthless dictator who murdered thousands of people.
5 The climbing team was completely fearless in the face of danger.
6 She was a tireless worker; she did not stop till everything was finished.
7 Their business went bankrupt two years ago and they are now penniless.
8 We waited for hours to be rescued and began to think it was hopeless.
9 The skier was helpless in the face of the avalanche.
10 I get very angry when I see mindless vandalism.

Exercise B Sample answers

1 That boy is quite brainless sometimes.
2 This injection should be painless.
3 This smokeless fuel doesn't cause too much environmental pollution.
4 The hapless driver drove straight into a lamp post.
5 It was a fruitless task, I'm afraid.
6 The horse cleared the gate with an effortless jump.
7 The landscape was the somewhat featureless.
8 Unfortunately, I found the official to be rather humourless.
9 I'm not continuing in this thankless task.
10 He was a heartless criminal and fully deserved his sentence.

Housewives' Choice?

Exercise A

1 It is argued by Murdock that certain jobs are universally done by women.
2 It is maintained by Murdock that the hunting is always done by men.
3 In the Soviet Union most of the low paid jobs are done by women.
4 It was argued by Murdock that pregnancy was a handicap that weakened women.
5 It is believed that women are strengthened by having babies.
6 It can be assumed that most of the housework done in the Soviet Union is done by women.
7 In some cultures the heavy work is shared by men and women.
8 The cleaners were always supervised by male caretakers when I was at school.
9 It has been noticed that in medicine the highest positions are filled by men.
10 Only a certain amount of inequality was removed by the Equal Pay Act of 1975.

Exercise B Sample Answers

1 In Eastern Europe, the housework is done mainly by women.
2 In African cultures, work is divided quite differently.
3 In the 16th Century, trading was often done by women.
4 In the future, housework will probably be shared more fairly.
5 In the 19th Century, girls were taught many domestic skills at school.
6 In an ideal world, work would be fairly divided.
7 In Murdock's opinion, labour is divided on similar lines everywhere.
8 In my house, the boring jobs are usually done by my mother.
9 In general, low-status work tends to be done by women.
10 In my opinion, labour should be divided according to ability not sex.

The Fourth Estate

Exercise A

1 The killings took place in the south of Managua.
2 The murder took place on the night of February 9th.
3 The discussion(s) took place at the Annual General Meeting.
4 The conquest took place on September 28th, 1066.
5 The stabbing took place in a council flat last month.
6 The argument took place outside a nightclub.
7 The drilling took place seventy miles offshore.
8 The executions took place in the Tower of London.
9 The negotiations took place at a special meeting.
10 The performance took place at Stratford.

Exercise B

1 I dislike cooking.
2 He loved power.
3 They absolutely loathe each other.
4 She really likes Italians.
5 The youngsters deeply distrusted authority.
6 They should understand the situation.
7 Those children greatly respected their parents.
8 I strongly suspect foul play.
9 We don't fear heights.
10 Do you dread failure?

Grammar Exercises: Keys *Interpretations in English*

Television is Watching You!

Exercise A
1. You mustn't walk on the grass; they have planted bulbs there.
2. You needn't walk on the grass; there's room on the pavement.
3. I needn't stay up to see the film; I can easily video it.
4. I mustn't miss *Neighbours* today - it's the final episode!
5. You mustn't drink that, it's poison.
6. You needn't drink it if you don't like it.
7. She mustn't forget her passport when she goes to the USA.
8. She needn't take her passport when she goes to the Isle of Man.
9. You mustn't drive at 50 mph in a built-up area.
10. You needn't drive fast; we aren't late.

Exercise B Sample answers
1. When you take a lot of wine through customs you must declare it.
2. If you want to buy stamps you need to go to a Post Office.
3. Anyone who visits Venice must leave their car.
4. If your passport's been stolen you need to report it.
5. If she intends to study at Oxford University she must pass her exams.
6. People who want to get *Sky* TV must buy a satellite dish.
7. Before one buys a house one usually needs to get a mortgage.
8. When you drive into a built-up area you must slow down.
9. If you ride a motorbike in Britain you need to wear a crash helmet.
10. Before you can get antibiotics in Britain you must obtain a doctor's prescription.

Soft Sell

Exercise A Sample answers
1. A manufacturer is someone who makes products.
2. A product is something that is sold.
3. An adman is someone who works for an advertising agency.
4. A client is someone who employs an advertising agency.
5. The tease is an advertising technique that does not mention the name of the product.
6. An advertising agency is a company that designs advertising material to promote products.
7. A billboard is a large poster which advertises a product.
8. A market researcher is a man or woman who interviews consumers to collect information about various products.
9. Levi 501s are jeans which are popular with young people.
10. Public Relations Officers are people who are employed to put forward the best possible image of a company or other organisation.

Exercise B

1 A product which has no profit margin but attracts customers is called a loss leader.
2 A person who designs advertising ideas is sometimes called a visualiser.
3 A persuasive talk that is delivered by a salesperson is called a sales pitch.
4 An association which monitors standards and infringements is known as a watchdog.
5 A person who lends out money at extortionate rates of interest is called a loan shark.
6 A sales technique that is particularly aggressive is known as the hard sell.
7 The advertising style that does not mention the name of the product is called the tease.
8 Someone who comes to your house uninvited to sell you something is called a door-to-door salesman.
9 An accident which involves a large number of fatalities is officially called a disaster.
10 A firm that specialises in analysing the success of advertising campaigns is called a market research company.

Murderers or Martyrs?

Exercise A Sample answers

1 He went to the consulate to get his work permit renewed.
2 He had to get the car insured for his wife to drive.
3 I desperately needed to get my hair cut.
4 I shall get the house valued by the Estate Agents.
5 We'll soon need to get the piano tuned.
6 You really ought to get that suit dry cleaned.
7 We'd better get the TV fixed before Christmas.
8 The secretary had to get the letters signed by the boss.
9 I can get this tooth capped on the NHS.
10 It's important to get the cash transferred.

Exercise B

1 I got my work permit renewed every year.
2 I had to get the car serviced.
3 She thought about getting the ring valued.
4 They wanted to get the roof seen to as soon as possible.
5 She got her hair permed at Gino's.
6 He wanted to get his glasses mended.
7 He considered getting the loft insulated.
8 I got my visa extended at the consulate.
9 Was she able to get the dress altered? (Could she get the dress altered?)
10 I got my wheel clamped for illegal parking.

Grammar Exercises: Keys   *Interpretations in English*

Defence of the Realm

Exercise A
1. He's quite intelligent, but he can't concentrate.
2. She's rather untidy I'm afraid.
3. I'm quite certain you never told me.
4. She's quite fast at typing, but her shorthand is rather slow.
5. It's quite true; I've forgotten.
6. It's a nice house, quite well decorated though it's in a rather noisy neighbourhood.
7. I'm rather disappointed in the car, to be honest.
8. I'm always rather hesitant when I drive in France and I find the centre of Paris quite impossible.
9. I thought he looked quite attractive but his conversation turned out to be rather boring.
10. My children are getting rather too good at saying what they think.

Exercise B
1. She thinks the concept of unilateral disarmament is rather unrealistic.
2. As a military power, the USSR has always been quite dominant.
3. To a lot of people, the concept of nuclear war is absolutely unacceptable.
4. The old-style conventional warfare was quite different.
5. Nowadays most people think a war between USA and USSR is somewhat unlikely.
6. The amount of money spent on weapons is quite incredible.
7. The recent talks between USSR and USA have been very encouraging.
8. The idea of third world countries holding nuclear weapons is rather frightening.
9. Many people think pacifists are somewhat weak.
10. To others, the pacifists are quite right.

This is I.T.!

Exercise A
1. I'm afraid I don't share your interest in computer programming.
2. Computers are now indispensible. The reason for this is their accuracy and speed of operation.
3.* Computers do not have the solution to most management problems.
4. This mainframe can make contact with other terminals all over the world.
5. There is no direct link between my micro and his workstation.
6. Hal could reply to any of the crew's questions in normal English.
7. There has been a fall in the cost of software recently.
8. Your reasons for learning about writing programs are quite different from mine.
9. There is a lot of difference between ASSEMBLY and COBOL.
10. There is a huge difference in price between the Amstrad and the IBM.

Interpretations in English   Grammar Exercises: Keys

Exercise B   Sample Answers

1 I'm interested in information technology.
2 I spend it all on computer games.
3 All the fuss was over nothing.
4 He is staying at a hotel in Bradford.
5 She is staying in Sofia.
6 I've just got up to page eleven.
7 Can you get it finished in two or three days?
8 My friend works for the National Trust.
9 He's working under the foreman.
10 They're employed by Olivetti.

Training for Life?

Exercise A

1 They used to play lacrosse as well.
2 I used to watch Children's Hour as well.
3 They used to have to wear caps as well.
4 You used to need Latin as well.
5 They used to have to learn needlework and ironing as well.
6 They used to read them the Bible as well.
7 They used to be able to claim training allowance as well.
8 You used to be able to do Spanish as well.
9 You used to need German as well.
10 You used to get a job as well.

Exercise B   Sample Answers

1 My son used to be enthusiastic about school but now he seems disillusioned.
2 The youngsters used to expect to get a job at the end of a youth training programme but now they expect a period of unemployment.
3 There used to be corporal punishment in most British schools but now it's illegal.
4 Teachers used to be drawn almost exclusively from the middle classes but now they are from all sorts of backgrounds.
5 Careers Officers used to offer a wide range of job possibilities but now they are very limited in what they can offer.
6 It used to be easy to go and work in, say, Australia but now you need to have a job to go to in advance.
7 You used to see dozens of jobs advertised in the Job Centres but now they are quite scarce.
8 There used to be a religious service every day in almost all schools but now this is the exception rather than the rule.
9 Most British schools used to insist on a strict uniform but now a lot of children wear what they like to school.
10 I used to tell the children: 'Your schooldays are the best days of your life', but now I'm not so sure.

unit.eight/nine

Tomorrow's World?

Exercise A
1 If the sea gets too polluted the fish will die.
2 If too many nitrates are allowed to flow into the sea the phytoplankton will increase.
3 If the Queen feels strongly about the latest report she will speak out.
4 If the sea is too badly poisoned it won't recover.
5 If action is taken immediately the sea won't die.
6 If the Humber is cleaned up the number of fish will be able to increase.
7 If the Avon gets too polluted most of its fish won't be able to survive.
8 If the North Sea is not rescued soon the fishermen won't be able to survive.
9 If European governments act fast the situation won't get worse.
10 If the British government continues to ignore the problem the situation won't be able to be reversed.

Exercise B Sample Answers
1 Once she tries that wine she won't leave it alone.
2 Once they start arguing they'll never stop.
3 Once he starts crawling he'll be an absolute menace.
4 Once we get settled into our flat we'll be able to spend more time with your parents.
5 Once he realises they are married he'll stop pestering her.
6 Once you start driving to work you'll understand how stressful it is.
7 Once they know you're leaving the atmosphere will improve.
8 Once she learns to open the door you'll have to watch her.
9 Once they get on television their career will really take off.
10 Once you get used to it you'll find it's better than your old one.